HARDWORKING FAITH

BUILDING FAITH FOR GLOBAL MISSIONS

THOMAS PAINO

ISBN # 978-0-9753725-9-3

Cover by Cabello Associates

Printed in the United States of America

HARDWORKING FAITH

BUILDING FAITH FOR GLOBAL MISSIONS

Dedicated to
My wife of over sixty-three years
Lois Marie Paino

TABLE OF CONTENTS

FOREWORD

DURING our 45-plus years of ministry, Joyce and I have been blessed to meet and rub shoulders with many of God's great champions: Our parents, the Herman Johnsons, and the Charles Dentons; my preaching brothers Dan and Joe; Vic Trimmer; Mark and Huldah Buntain; Bernard and Doris Johnson; Bob and Hazel Hoskins; Charles and Mary Greenaway; Jerry and Karen Parlsey; David and Sharon Burdine, just to name a few.

However, Tom and Lois Paino stand out to us in a very special way. First of all, Dr. Paino was one of our supporting pastors while we were missionaries in Portugal, building the Bible school there. Secondly, he became a mentor to me in the whole new arena of financing huge missionary projects.

As we have traveled thousands of miles together, walking the streets of many foreign capitals, and combining our efforts to build Bible schools and churches around the globe, I continue to learn from the master teacher—Dr. Paino.

His life and godly example are set forth in this book, to be emulated by every person. The principles and practices he sets forth are to be studied and applied. The story of his life's work is not only an inspiration for others to learn from, but it is a pattern to be followed.

As you read this book may God plant the seed of increasing passion to fulfill the Great Commission – Go, Win, Teach – that's priority one!

Tom Paino lives his life that way: Action NOW!

Sam Johnson
Executive Director
Priority One

PREFACE

I BELIEVE God has a purpose for the life of every person. When we discover that purpose and dedicate ourselves to fulfilling it, each of us can make a difference in our world. That's what this book is about: Touching our world in some special way.

My greatest desire as pastor of Lakeview Church in Indianapolis for thirty-eight years was to make an impact on more lives than I could touch inside the four walls of the building. Our son, Troy, wrote a book on the history of the first seventy-five years of Lakeview—from 1918 to 1993. The theme of the celebration and the title of the book was *Touching Our World With His Hands*. It was a challenge to the congregation to work and pray together, keeping our eye on the purpose that God had for us to make a difference.

I share with you in this book how I determined the will of God for my life and the circumstances that brought me face to face with that calling from a very early age. Fulfilling the Great Commission was something I took very seriously, but for many years I wrestled with what my involvement in the plan of God was to be. I knew that these were solemn days, living as we do on the edge of an atomic volcano, the world population increasing with explosive force, with millions living undernourished and dying unevangelized. I knew we needed direction, we needed to know for sure where we were going and what we could do about it. We needed to understand the times in which we were living.

This is the story of how those questions and challenges had a profound effect on my life and how that vision carried me through some very difficult times. The Word of God presents an overview of the plan of God, and our place in it, but one needs a special vision from the Lord. This is what occurred in the life of Isaiah when the prophet saw the Lord of glory (Isaiah 6). The dazzling rays of light from that magnificent vision penetrated and searched the darkened corners of his heart and changed his life forever.

The apostle Paul was nearing the end of his life of service to the Lord Jesus when he found himself standing before King Agrippa. In his defense, he described his experience on the Damascus Road, of how he saw a light from heaven and received a commission from the Lord Himself. Then he made a statement which revealed one of the secrets of his life, a statement that has stirred every generation since: "Whereupon, O King Agrippa, I was not disobedient to the heavenly vision" (Acts 26:19).

Paul had an all-consuming purpose in his life. My prayer is that as you read this testimonial, you will discover the purpose of God for your life, and in finding it, you will go on to be *His Hands Touching Our World* in some special way.

ACKNOWLEDGMENTS

I **WANT** to thank each one who has helped make this book possible, first of all to the members of ActioNow, who have faithfully stood with us in their generous support from year to year. Without these people of vision and commitment nothing you will read in these pages would have been possible.

Secondly, Sam Johnson kept encouraging me to put in writing an account of the many priority missions projects we have been involved with over the years. I am grateful for his support in many ways. Dan Johnson has taken the time to help prepare the material for publication. Jack Strom went over the material several times, making suggestions, editing and pointing out the many times I had repeated myself.

My son, Dr. Troy Paino, provided valuable insights and assisted with editing to make the story more readable. Eddy Cabello gave helpful advice and encouragement to make the book attractive.

My wife, Lois, helped me with sentence structure, and for many years has traveled with me to sixty different nations of the world.

I have gleaned many quotes over the years from different sources and have sought to make proper acknowledgement to those responsible. Where it has not been possible to locate a source, I have indicated by quotation marks material which is not original.

MAKING A
DIFFERENCE IN OUR WORLD

258 Priority Missions Projects . . . 178 by ActioNow

Faith looks across the storm, it does not doubt
Or stop to look at clouds and things without.
Faith does not question why when all God's ways
Are hard to understand, but trusts and prays.
It seeks the greatest gift and asks not sight,
It does not need to see, He is its light.
Above the tempest's roar it hears His voice;
And, with its hand in His, faith can rejoice.
It fears no clouds, or wind that it can bring,
Faith looks across the storm and still can sing.

I

PREPARATION FOR VISION

*No one discovers new lands without
consenting to lose sight of the shore
for a very long time.*

I WAS sitting in the Tokyo airport with my wife, Lois, and missionary friend, Sam Johnson. Lois and I, together with another couple, had just concluded a five-day visit to China. We had gone to China to witness what God is doing there, and, as Executive Director of ActioNow, I was interested in seeing what opportunities there were to sponsor priority missions projects in that nation of a billion people.

Earlier we had flown to the Philippines where we met up with Sam Johnson. Five days in the Philippines were filled with activity and travel, including a six-hour trek up the mountains where the Asia/Pacific Theological Seminary is located in a lovely city called Baguio.

One year prior to this time, two of us from ActioNow had made this same trip where we met with Dr. Cagle, president of the school. He showed us pictures of two faculty buildings the school desperately needed. When I asked about the cost of these buildings, the president told me that the missionaries would raise the money to purchase the land if our organization would provide funds for construction of the buildings.

Now we were in Baguio to dedicate these facilities that would house four professor families. It was during the rainy season, the clouds hung low and visibility was very limited, but at dedication time the clouds opened up and the sun shown through; it was a beautiful sight. The buildings are on top of a mountain, fifty-two hundred feet high, looking down over the valley below.

Two duplexes, Asia/Pacific Theological Seminary, Bagiuo, Philippines. These facilities allow seminar faculty to bring their families during the school year, also provides dormitory space for additional students.

We had accomplished our mission. But the next morning, the president asked to talk to Sam, David Wagner, missionary contractor, and myself. He showed us plans to expand the library at a cost of $1.25 million dollars. Through a ministry organization called Priority One, Sam Johnson raises funds for missions projects, just as I have done for the past fifteen years with a group of business people. The two of us took a step of faith and made a commitment over the next two years to raise the money necessary to complete the library project.

From Baguio, we returned to Manila. A typhoon had gone through the night before. Many of the villages were flooded and we traveled through water over the highways for many miles. A full schedule awaited us as we arrived in the city. At 10:30 a.m. we were to conduct a service and dedicate a five-color printing press that ActioNow had helped purchase for the International Correspondence Institute that provides literature for schools, churches and religious organizations for many countries in the Asia Pacific region.

The purchase of this piece of equipment was another miracle, beyond our expectations. David Wagner and I had visited the ICI facilities because ActioNow had provided funds to enlarge the building which houses the literature that is sent out to many countries. Missionary Mike Williams thanked us for the needed space that was provided.

I have a habit of asking questions, so when Mike suggested the mission could save hundreds of thousands of dollars a year if they had their own printing press, I found myself involved in another program that could change lives for Christ. I asked how much money it would take to purchase a good printing press. When he told me it would cost about $900,000, I knew it would take a lot more faith than I had at that moment to make such a commitment. "Get a price from the manufacturer," I said, "and perhaps we can find other organizations that will work with us to purchase the equipment."

We learned that we could purchase a five-color printing press for $750,000. That's when I received a call from David Wagner with interesting news. The printing company, renting space in his building, had purchased a new five-color press, but the business had floundered, forcing them into bankruptcy. They walked out, leaving everything behind.

"Lock the doors, David," I said. "Let's deal directly with the bank and find out what it will take to purchase this press." Within a week of negotiations, we had purchased the press and all the equipment that goes with it for $165,000 – a million-dollar piece of equipment. ActioNow stepped forward to make the purchase possible and there was much rejoicing on August 5, 2006, when we dedicated the new printing press.

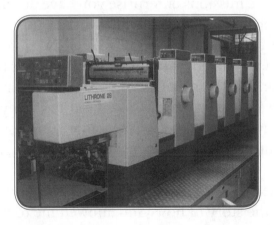

A million dollar, five-color printing press purchased by ActioNow, provides literature for ICI program, Bible colleges and schools throughout Asia.

Following the dedication, we moved to the chapel of Bethel Bible College in Manila and dedicated a beautiful dormitory, dining hall and kitchen, again, made possible by ActioNow. From there we went directly to the airport and flew a thousand miles south to Davao, Philippines, where a couple were ministering to four thousand boys and girls every weekend. They conducted six services a day, with seven hundred children in each service, plus many parents and others, in a small rented building with bleachers up to the ceiling. They showed us land that had been purchased and asked if we could finance a building during the next year. Their goal was to provide facilities to minister to seventy-five hundred boys and girls by the end of the year.

With these victories and challenges going through our minds, sitting in the Tokyo airport, Sam Johnson said, "Dr. Paino, you need to write the story of how God has led you, both in the church you pastored for thirty-eight years and the worldwide missions enterprise you have developed both at the church and through ActioNow."

Over the years others have suggested putting into print what God has enabled us to do, but I always felt inadequate for the task. But Sam persisted, "Your children and your grandchildren need to know how God has led you as you built a great church, and at the same time established a missions outreach that has touched the world. And others will receive inspiration and find direction for their lives, showing them how to make a difference in our world."

So this is the story of how God allowed me to be involved in the building of a strong missions church, then after fifty years of pastoring, to continue with a ministry that raises finances for priority missions projects around the world, through an organization called ActioNow. Over two hundred and fifty missions projects have become a reality of a God-given call and challenge to my heart that the "Go ye" of the Great Commission was meant for me to obey.

Something Otis Keener said confirmed what God had been dealing with me about for many years. The missionary evangelist, speaking at the church I pastored, said, "Any church or person not involved in fulfilling the Great Commission fails out of ignorance or willful disobedience."

"Not every Christian is called to be a missionary," theologian and pastor, John Piper writes. "But every follower of Christ is called to be a world Christian. A world Christian is someone who is so gripped by the glory of God and the glory of His global purpose that he chooses to align himself with God's mission to fill the earth with the knowledge of His glory. Everything a world Christian does, he does with a view to the hallowing of God's name and the coming of God's kingdom among all the people of the earth."

Robertson McQuilkin, veteran missionary statesman, said, "The key to completing the Great Commission is the energizing power of the Holy Spirit, but the key to unleashing the power is obedient faith, and I'm not all that confident that the American church is connecting with Him on those terms."

I trust that as you read this book you will be one of those that will say, "I will connect." My prayer is, "Lord, what is Your will for my generation? How do You want my life to fit into Your plan for my times?"

As I write this book, at eighty-three, I still make that my daily prayer. And God is still enabling me to raise a million and a half dollars a year through the giving partners of ActioNow for priority missions projects.

If we are not the generation of Christians to see the fulfillment of the Unfinished Task—we who posess more data on global harvest than any previous generation, we who stand on the shoulders of twenty centuries of missionary giants, WHO ELSE IS? If we fail to throw all our heart and energies into the global harvest now, as the Holy Spirit is moving over the world, WHO ELSE WILL? No generation has ever seen so many doors of opportunity open so wide. WHEN WILL THERE BE A MORE OPPORTUNE TIME?

I am not suggesting that we run off in all directions with mere human enthusiasm, fueled by a noble cause. I am urging that we be imbued with the spirit of the sons of Issachar, "who understood the times and knew what the people of God should do" (1 Chronicles 12:32). May we possess an understanding of the times and a clear sense of what these times demand. This is no time to be idle. It is a time to do what it takes to fulfill our mission in the Spirit's strength, in the Father's ripe vineyard, for the honor of the Son, Jesus Christ.

We must remember that harvest time is seasonal.

Many years ago, Lois and I pastored in a small farming community in southwest Minnesota. One of the members of our church was a farmer who was meticulous about everything he did. He maintained his equipment in excellent condition. He spent the winters making sure that every piece of equipment was ready when spring arrived. He cultivated his fields so thoroughly that you couldn't find a weed in his hundreds of acres. It was a pleasure to look out over his fields of wheat and corn.

We had another farmer in the church who waited until the last minute to do what was necessary to plant or harvest the fields. One fall he was late in getting in his corn crop. When a storm came in, very high winds blew most of the sixty acres down on the ground. He came to my home with tears saying he was going to lose the crop and the farm.

Being a young pastor, full of energy, I said, "Let's go out and pick the corn by hand." That would be impossible, he said, but I insisted on doing it. His son drove the tractor, pulling the wagon, as I began to pick the corn while the farmer worked on the equipment. We saved the crop, but the farmer was still working on the corn picker when I finished the job. There's a lesson there: Let's not make the mistake of working on machinery when it's harvest time.

Urgency is the word when it's harvest time. Jesus said, "I must work the works of Him who sent Me while it is day; the night is coming when no man can work" (John 9:4).

Fear swept through the streets of Amsterdam on May 10, 1940, as Hitler's armies invaded the Netherlands, Belgium and Luxembourg. Europe was in the grip of World War II. Three days later, Winston Churchill stood before the British Parliament and passionately declared, "I have nothing to offer but blood, toil, tears and sweat. You ask, what is our policy? I will say, it is to wage war by sea, by land and air, with all our might and with all the strength God can give us."

Churchill had a passion for victory. There is a far greater battle raging today, a battle between the forces of light and darkness, a battle for the souls of men and women. How seriously do we take the Great Commission that our Lord left us? Oswald J. Smith, pastor of the Peoples Church in Toronto, had a heart for God and a heart for missions. In his book, *The Passion for Souls*, he asks, "Why should anyone hear the Gospel twice until everyone has heard it once?"

"Some people want to live within the sound of the church bell," said C.T. Studd, "but I want to run a rescue shop within a yard of hell." The young Englishman, born to wealth, backed up that statement by giving away his last penny and spending his life in Africa preaching the Gospel. C.T. Studd was made of the same stuff as the apostle Paul, who never lost the wonder of his experience on the Damascus road or the sight of the heavenly vision.

II

VISION UNFOLDING

Missionaries are not made by crossing the sea; but by seeing the cross.

I WAS seventeen years old when I entered Central Bible College in Springfield, Missouri, in 1941. God had been dealing with me from a very early age and I felt a definite call to the ministry. Perhaps fueling that call was the fact that my parents were pioneer preachers. I had witnessed the hand of God in the lives of my parents, who had received their calling under the ministry of Mrs. Woodworth-Etter, whom God used in a ministry of miracles across the United States.

My mother and father began their ministry under tents and in brush-arbor meetings, establishing churches in town after town, until finally they were called to Indianapolis to pastor the Woodworth-Etter Tabernacle. The tabernacle became the headquarters for the evangelist, where she held meetings four times a year. After her death, the church went through a troubled period. By the time my parents returned to their home church in 1933 just a handful of people were left.

I was just a boy of nine, but I remember how God visited us in a special way. Over the next several years a strong church was established and many young people found Christ and went out into the ministry. I was one of them. I was always sensitive to the things of God and challenged every time a missionary came through our city. While studying for the ministry, I often rose early to wait on the Lord. As I did so, the challenge of missions was ever before me.

When I graduated from college in 1944, I thought I might be called to military service as World War II was still being fought. But God had other plans. A serious relationship had developed with a young lady from Wisconsin and a September wedding date had been planned. The dean of the school called us into his office one day and asked if we were serious about getting married. When we assured him we were, he told us a pastor in Goose Creek, Texas, wanted us to come as youth pastors, and suggested we move up our wedding date.

We were thrilled at the prospect, but the thrill was short-lived. A week before graduation and our wedding, word came that the church had decided to go into a building program and would be unable to afford a youth pastor. So our journey of faith began the very first day of our married life.

We were asked to go to East Chicago, Indiana, and pastor a storefront church on Main Street. We were happy to have a place to go to and grateful for a weekly salary of twenty dollars. We learned valuable lessons during those days and saw God do some special things in the lives of the people, and soon our little sixty-seven-seat room was filled. We purchased land but were unable to build because building material was difficult to find during those wartime years.

Feeling we had done all we could under the circumstances, living in a room and a half behind the church, with little room for our first son, Thomas III (Tommy), we decided to leave in the fall of 1946.

We were invited to St. James, a small country town in southwestern Minnesota. Here we learned skills in building, as the church had never been completed. We laid a floor in the auditorium, built a nursery, finished the basement and built classrooms for the Sunday School. God knew I would need this experience later on. Our salary increased and we were now making thirty-five dollars a week. We spent four wonderful years in St. James watching the church grow, learning people skills and developing personal ministry. And here our second child, a little girl, Susan Kay was born.

The next step in our journey brought us back to Covington, Indiana, to serve the church my father had started in 1931 before returning to Indianapolis to pastor the Woodworth-Etter Tabernacle. I had attended the second and third grades of school in Covington. We found the church in great turmoil and wondered why God had called us into such a situation, but again, it was a learning experience. God was teaching me how to deal with problems, trying to bring unity out of chaos. Over the next year and a half we witnessed God's blessing and saw the church come together, and God was preparing us for a future ministry.

The next four years found us in Evansville, Indiana, where once again we found a church in need of healing. God gave us wisdom in dealing with situations far beyond our ability. We developed a love for the people as we worked and prayed together, believing that the Lord would do a special work. But God was doing more than helping these congregations, He was preparing Lois and me for a greater ministry. A second son was added to our family in Evansville, Timothy Dean.

In 1956, because of my mother's health problems, my folks asked us to come to Indianapolis and join them as co-pastors of the home church. The Woodworth-Etter Tabernacle had burned to the ground, and a new building had been constructed and renamed West Side Gospel Tabernacle. Our first task upon arrival in Indianapolis was to organize the church and prepare it for growth. Not only did we experience growth in the church, but we added two new members to our family, Tracy Randall and Troy Dale.

It was not long until we invited my brother-in-law and sister, Harold and Edwina Duncan, to come to Indianapolis and join the staff. They served with us for the next five years, during which time we expanded the church's facilities, enlarging the auditorium to accommodate the growth. For the next several years the church enjoyed continuous revival.

My father always had a heart for the elderly, especially for those confined to their homes. We found that many senior citizens were kept without proper care. I can remember my father taking groceries to their homes and looking after them. It was at this time that the Lord began speaking to my heart about doing something for these forgotten people.

There were no nursing homes in our city at that time. I knew of a man in Minneapolis who had built a number of nursing homes, so my brother-in-law and I flew to Minneapolis to visit these centers and learn what we could about their operation. We returned home committed to building a facility to care for senior citizens who needed care.

I soon learned that there were three elements necessary to accomplish what was in our hearts at that time. It was imperative that we had a *vision* for the task. I had a vision for the church, I knew the direction I was trying to lead the congregation. But did I have a clear vision for the task of reaching out to hurting people in need of loving care? Was this to be a part of the ministry to which God had called us?

In addition to a vision, I needed to know more about the *mission*. Mission has to do with one's calling. When one is challenged, and trying times come, you have to know God has called you. To be certain of the mission requires time to wait upon God, visit with people, and talk with professionals about plans and finances.

The third element is *resources*. There must be spiritual undergirding, physical and material undergirding. Where would we go for help? What about finances? We strongly felt that we wanted to proceed with a place for the elderly. In addition to this, we had outgrown our church facilities and needed to relocate and build for a growing congregation.

We went to the church board to share our vision, but the majority of them were not in favor of the church getting involved in a nursing home. We had no money and I realized I had failed to transfer my vision to them. It was too risky, we were told. But God had laid it on my heart and I could not turn back. I knew I would be walking alone except for the support of my father, Thomas Paino, Sr. God's faith needed to be dropped into my heart.

This book is my way of taking you on that journey to fulfill the vision God gave me. The vision included not only a ministry to the elderly in need of loving care, but also the building of new church facilities, fulfilling what God had laid on my heart as a young man. I had a desire to be involved in missions in some special way but did not feel a definite call to a particular country, so I resolved to build a church with a mission's heart. This monumental task would require that miracle of faith.

THE MIRACLE OF FAITH

If without faith I lose my way in darkness,
And without faith my hopes and dreams would fail,
Then give me faith to flood my way with brightness,
And give me faith to see my hopes prevail.

Almighty God, the source of my salvation,
Impart to me your miracle of faith.
Let faith remain a bulwark for all seasons,
Let faith be always equal to the hour.
Be not concerned with earthling doubts or reasons,
Fly on the wings of faith's eternal power.

III

FAITH AT WORK

The poet, Browning, wrote that our reach should exceed our grasp, "or what's a heaven for?" Faith inspires us to reach beyond our grasp, to do daring things. Faith may lead us into places and situations that logic says are impossible, like Abraham moving out into the unknown, or Schweitzer leaving the comfortable world of music and theological inquiry to build a hospital in the African jungle.

AFTER much prayer, I decided to form a separate nonprofit corporation and continue the journey that would ultimately lead to the establishment of a global ministry. The first thing we needed was land, enough land to build a convalescent center and, later, a church. We located fifteen acres at the cloverleaf of an expressway that circled the city of Indianapolis. It was an ideal location for people to find from any place in the city. Providentially, a "for sale" sign had just been posted on the property. The selling price was $45,000. That's not a lot of money in today's economy, but in the early 1960s that was an enormous amount of money, especially when you didn't have any.

What appeared to be an impossible hurdle proved to be the place another step of faith came into play. "We need to know God's will," my father said. "I'm going to go out and talk to two people, neither of whom attends our church. If each of them gives a thousand dollars, we'll take that as an indication that God is leading us to purchase the property."

First, my father went to a funeral director and shared our vision. The man immediately offered a thousand dollars to help build the convalescent center. Then my father went to a lady who owned a small drug store and told her what we wanted to do. "I want to be one of the first to make an investment," she said, and wrote a check for a thousand dollars. My father returned that afternoon, handed me $2,000 and said, "I believe you are to move forward and purchase that piece of land."

I went to the owner of the land and said, "I want to purchase your property. I'll give you $2,000 today and pay the balance in sixty days." The man hesitated for a moment, then agreed. I was confident I could go to the bank and borrow the funds necessary to finalize the sale. That's when a big road block appeared on the journey of faith.

Although my father and mother had pastored the church in Indianapolis for twenty-five years, they had never established credit with a bank. My folks were from the old school where you paid cash for everything. If you needed a car, you saved until you had the money. If there was a utility bill, you took up an offering and had the treasurer go downtown and pay it. Since there had been no credit established, bank after bank turned me down.

I had sixty days to come up with the money to complete the sale of the property. No bank would help and I didn't have the backing of the church and I faced a bleak situation. We needed the land for the convalescent center, but most of it would be used to house the new facilities of our growing church.

At a time like this you need to know that you have an avenue to God, so I began to pray. I prayed earnestly as the sixty days drew to a close. Then it happened. God spoke to my heart about a man who had been in the ministry in California. I knew of him, but did not know him personally, had never met him. I knew he had left the ministry and gone into the insurance business and was now president of a small insurance company in Gary, Indiana. I was impressed to go and see him and talk to him about helping us purchase the land.

I felt so strongly about it that one day I got in my car and drove a hundred and twenty miles to Gary. I found his office and walked inside. I had not called for an appointment but told the receptionist I had come to see the president. After introducing myself, I told him my story and asked if he would loan me the money we needed for ninety days. I had never met the man, he knew nothing about me to my knowledge, but he wrote me a check for $45,000.

During this time, I had hired an architect who was busy drawing plans for a one-hundred-forty-bed convalescent center, later to be increased to one-hundred-eighty beds. I was certain that with the land paid for and architectural drawings underway, the banks would be happy to loan us money, but I had no success as I found myself getting deeper and deeper in debt.

How many times someone came by offering to help! Some of these would-be helpers were out to make a quick buck, and we wasted a lot of time until we were forced one more time to look to the Lord for guidance and help. I knew God was leading us and would provide for us because our ministry was geared toward helping hurting people.

Just when it looked hopeless, another miracle occurred. I remembered a man who had come to my office one time and inquired about our work. He wondered if we were getting ready to build and expand our program at the church. When I told him we had no plans to do anything at that time, he gave me his card and said, "If you ever need money for a building program, I can help you."

I thanked him, he left the office and I threw his card in a desk drawer and forgot about it. But God remembered, and now reminded me of that visit and I went looking for that card. I made a call to Mr. Clarence Ridenour in Dayton, Ohio and referred to his visit to my office two years before. When I explained what I was doing, he promised to come over and visit with me.

The very next day Mr. Ridenour was in my office. When I laid out the plans for the convalescent center and discussed the estimated cost of construction, he assured me there would be no problem in raising the money. He said he would draw up a Prospectus and said he had clients ready to purchase large sums of the bonds.

A bond issue was soon ready. The one thing that made me hesitate was that the cost would be ten percent of the program, but since I had no other recourse I moved forward, believing that God would help us meet the high payments. I was confident that once the center was completed, and we were in business, we would be able to meet our obligations. Within a matter of days, the money arrived in our account and we moved forward with construction.

There always seemed to be another obstacle as we moved forward. Work had just begun when we learned there was no sewer line to our property. We would have to put in our own sewer system or tie into one of the conservancies in our area. I inquired of the Speedway conservancy to see if they would run a line to our property, but was told they would have had to run a new line one and a half miles to our site. They weren't interested in doing that, so we went to Ben Davis conservancy with the same question and received a similar reply; they were not interested in extending their system.

We knew we would never get a building permit without resolving this problem. It was about this time that one of the men in our church told me that he knew the president of the Ben Davis conservancy and offered to talk to him on our behalf. The president promised to help us get permission to connect to their lines on the condition that we bear the expense of running the sewer line under the railroad with a lift station. I attended the next board meeting of the conservancy where the matter was discussed.

When it came to a vote, we were turned down. It was then the president spoke up and said, "I promised this preacher that if he came to this meeting we would grant permission to install the sewer system according to city regulations, and, as a favor, I would like for this board to reconsider its vote." They reconsidered and voted in favor of our moving forward with the provision that we maintain the system for ten years before turning it over to the city of Indianapolis.

With the first step to moving forward accomplished, we proceeded to get bids from three contractors. The bids came in at $100,000. Again, in the middle of the 1960s, that was a great amount of money. I contacted one of the contractors I knew personally and offered him the job. "But I don't have any money." I said, "I'll pay you every Friday for the work you've done, and if I can't pay, you stop the job." He said, "I have never taken a contract on these terms before, but I have faith that you will pay as I move along through the job."

Now another miracle occurred. The contractor started digging and wasn't two days into the job when a businessman came to my office and asked if we were putting in a sewer line that would run to edge of our property. When I assured him we were, and had already started on the project, he said, "Can I connect to your line?"

"I don't see any problem with that," I replied. He told me that he had put down good faith money on the forty acres adjoining ours and planned to put in four hundred apartment units. He asked how much it would cost to tie into our line. I had no idea what I should charge to tie into the sewer line with four hundred units, but I said, "You can tie in for $33,000, but you will have to pay me by Friday of this week."

He thought I was kidding him, but I assured him the only way he could connect was to pay the money up front. With that he stormed out of my office only to return the next day with his lawyer and a contract, and a check for the amount I had requested.

With money in my hand, I went to the contractor and said, "Keep on digging, I've got enough money for the next couple of weeks." I knew that this money would soon run out and I would need help again. That's when the businessman who was building apartments returned to my office. "I can't make it with four hundred units," he explained, "I need to build eight hundred units. What will it cost to connect the extra units to the sewer line?"

"Bob," I answered, "it will cost you $17,000 for the extra units." He said, "I suppose you want the money by Friday." I assured him I would like to have a check by the end of the week. I'm half way there, I thought. I did not know how God would supply the other half, but I knew He is always faithful.

By now, Bob was no stranger. Once again he came with a request: "I want to put in a strip mall on the front of my property. Can I connect these units to the sewer line, and if so, what will it cost?" I charged him $15,000 plus two houses on his property that had to be moved. He was to move them to our property, at his expense.

While installing the sewer line, a number of homes wanted to connect to our line. I charged $500 for each connection. Two gas stations connected for $5,000 each. Another developer connected his units for $25,000. By the time we were done, we had more than enough money to complete the work.

Why go to such lengths to trace the background of this ministry? It is to demonstrate how God was preparing us for the future. It would have been impossible to raise millions of dollars through ActioNow priority missions projects unless God had taught me how to walk by faith.

A TASK UNFINISHED

Facing a task unfinished, that drives us to our knees,
A need that, undiminished, rebukes our slothful ease,
We, who rejoice to know Thee, renew before Thy throne
The solemn pledge we owe Thee, to go and make Thee known.

Where other lords beside Thee hold their unhindered sway,
Where forces that defied Thee defy Thee still today,
With none to heed their crying for life and love and light,
Unnumbered souls are dying, and pass into the night.

We bear the torch that flaming fell from the hands of those
Who gave their lives proclaiming that Jesus died and rose;
Ours is the same commission, the same glad message ours;
Fired by the same ambition, to Thee we yield our pow'rs.

O Father, Who sustained them, O Spirit, Who inspired,
Savior, whose love constrained them to toil with zeal untired,
From cowardice defend us, from lethargy awake!
Forth on Thy errands send us to labor for They sake.

-Frank Houghton

IV

FAITH CHALLENGED

It is easier to serve God without a vision, easier to work for God without a call, because then you are not bothered by what God requires; common sense is your guide. You will be more leisure-hearted if you never realize the call of God. But if once you receive a commission from Jesus Christ, the memory of what God wants will always come like a goad; you will no longer be able to work for Him on the common-sense basis.

Oswald Chambers

OUR faith was challenged from the very beginning, but God enabled us to overcome every setback. First, we had to determine the will of God. What did He want us to do? Confirmation was provided as people stepped forward to make an investment. Finances came from unexpected sources when loaning institutions turned us down. Then we discovered there was no sewer line to the project, and two conservancies who could have helped turned a deaf ear to our request. Finding a contractor who would install the sewer system with nothing but a promise to pay every Friday, when we had no idea where the money would come from, stretched our faith even further. But once again, God opened a door that seemed to be closed.

A developer had put down earnest money on the forty acres adjoining ours with the intention of building a number of apartments. We met his need by allowing him to connect with our line, and he met our need by paying in advance, which enabled us to complete the sewer line without delay. Securing finances for construction of the center was now front and center, something the Lord had taken care of two years in advance.

We were on our way now to fulfilling the dream of providing a center where loving care could be administered to senior citizens in our community. There was one more hurdle: We still needed a permit. A man living in the neighborhood, who served on the city council, decided that it would not be a good thing to issue a permit, so he opposed us. We appealed the decision from the preliminary committee on three different occasions and were turned down each time. When our fourth appeal, to the full board of the city council, was turned down, I knew it was time for drastic action. I brought five-hundred members of our church—people who go to the polls on election day—to the next appeal and left with a permit.

When you know what you're doing is right, it's always too soon to quit. Winston Churchill, England's wartime prime minister, serves as an example of that principle. As a young journalist he was captured during the Boar War. He escaped two weeks later. His captors issued a wanted poster describing the young man:

ENGLISHMAN, 25 years old, 5 feet 8 inches tall, indifferent build, walks with a forward stoop, pale appearance, reddish-brown hair, small mustache, talks through his nose and cannot pronounce letter "s" properly.

This less-than-complimentary description didn't bother Winston Churchill as much as the price they had put on his head: 25 pounds. This made him furious because he knew he was worth more than they were offering (about $60). He went on to prove his worth to his country on more than one occasion. It was his character and not his physical appearance that made Winston Churchill a national treasure.

There was a stubborn streak in the man; he was a scrapper who refused to roll over and play dead when tyrants threatened. He was often knocked down, but refused to stay down, believing that a man who hangs on to hope can never be beaten. On June 4, 1940, with Britain's future at stake, Winston Churchill's bull-dog determination found expression in a famous speech:

"We shall go to on to the end, we shall fight on the seas and oceans, we shall fight with growing confidence and growing strength in the air; we shall defend our island whatever the cost may be; we shall fight in the streets, we shall fight in the hills; we shall never surrender."

We must possess this kind of passion if we are to make a difference in our world. Passion must become a driving force, infusing life with meaning, commitment and determination. Passion is that urge that calls for action, enabling others to lead bigger, richer and fuller lives; to create a better world. It is a spark that becomes a flame that becomes a blazing fire that stirs the soul.

It was this passion that has driven me to go places others were afraid to go, to try things others were afraid to try. This kind of compelling energy has driven me to do things some thought impossible.

One of the lessons learned early in my ministry was that nothing worth while is easy. I was soon to be reminded of that principle. We selected a contractor who didn't stay on the job, or pay attention to details. When a workman told me that the hallways in the building were narrower than required by law, and other plans weren't being followed, I had no recourse but to fire the contractor at a cost of $100,000 and hire one of his men to finish the building.

The convalescent center had been under construction for three or four months when Mr. Ridenour came to me and suggested we build the church facility simultaneously. "I'm sure I can raise the money," he said, "to do both projects at the same time." That sounded good to me, and I gave my consent, giving little thought to the fact that I would have to repay what I had borrowed. So we began the first phase of construction of Lakeview Church with all the usual frustrations such an endeavor entails.

It was an exciting day in 1968 when Lakeview Manor was completed and we entered a new phase of ministry that would eventually touch the lives of thousands over the next forty years. Those first years were a testing time as we embarked upon a business of this kind with little prior experience. Month by month we wondered how we would meet payroll, cover the mortgage, pay utility bills and all the other expenses involved in such a large undertaking.

At one of those critical times, the administrator came to my office and informed me that we had a payroll coming due, a mortgage payment to make, and no money in the bank. When I asked him what he suggested we do, he replied, "It's not my problem." With that I had to make a decision. "If this isn't your problem," I responded, "then I don't need you." I relieved the administrator of his responsibilities, believing that he was not effectively managing our facilities.

Now I needed two miracles. This all happened on a Tuesday, and that night was spent in prayer. I needed divine guidance to show me how to face this problem. The following night, after our midweek service, an usher came to me and said a Dr. Hancock would like to see me. Our church had befriended this man's daughter and brought her to church each Sunday. "Tom, are you in need of some money?" Dr. Hancock asked when we met. I looked at him and said, "Doctor, I have a very critical need coming up this Friday and I don't know how I will meet it."

"How much do you need?" he asked. I was afraid to tell him I needed $30,000. I thought it might sound better to tell him I needed $25,000. The doctor asked, "Can you use $35,000?" With that, he wrote me check for that amount. Again, at the last minute, the Lord was faithful. My faith had been challenged, but I knew the testing time was not over.

God continued to meet the financial pressure of starting a ministry with little experience and no money. Dr. Hancock came to my door on the thirtieth of every month for the next seven months with a check for $30,000. He told me it would be fine if I could repay it, but not to worry about it if unable to do so.

I am happy to report that over the next several years I was able to repay every dollar Dr. Hancock loaned me and before his death I had the privilege of leading him to the Lord. More about this good doctor a little later in the book.

Now we needed someone who knew accounting to come and work in our office, someone to pull everything together and help us survive the first year of operations. The only person I could think of was a young man by the name of Tom Tyson. My eldest son, Tommy, had gone to college with Tom and brought him home from college one weekend. I knew he had majored in accounting and might be the man we were looking for.

I called my son, who was in the army at the time, and asked if he knew where Tom Tyson was, and did he think he would be willing to come and work for us. I learned that Tom had been working for the government, but had just taken a new job with Scotts Fertilizer Company and moved to Ohio. "Dad, I don't think Tom would be interested," my son said, "because they have given him a good position and he has found a teaching job for his wife."

I spent a restless night, then arose early Sunday morning and went over to church. As I stood in the pulpit to deliver my message, I looked out over the congregation and saw Tom Tyson sitting there. I spoke up and said, "Tom, I don't know where you came from, but I need to talk to you after the service."

We got together at the convalescent home that afternoon and went over the books. "You're in deep trouble, Pastor Paino," he told me. I knew that. What I wanted was some answers. Tom suggested a firm in the city, Fowler and Suttle. Perhaps they could help. I felt led to ask Tom to come and work for me. That would be impossible, he informed me; he had just taken a new job and his wife was given a teaching position. Tom had come to pick up his wife who had gone to a reunion and he was to meet her in Indianapolis and return to Ohio.

On his way home, Tom recounted our visit with his wife, Lanita. He told her he had been invited to come to Indianapolis to serve as comptroller for the convalescent home and assume the position of youth minister at the church. "And what did you say?" Lanita asked. Tom responded that he told me it would be impossible to make such a change at this time.

"You turned Tom Paino down and didn't even pray about it?" Lanita, a tender-hearted person asked. That night they prayed together, and the next morning Tom Tyson told his boss about his visit to Indianapolis and his decision to resign from his new job. "Tom," his boss said, "we have spent thousands of dollars to get you moved and settled here, and there's no way I would let you leave—except for a church." The boss gave him two weeks pay, told him to pack his things and wished him well. That afternoon Tom Tyson went to work in Indianapolis.

The young man went through the books and found thousands of dollars that had not been collected. A number of families whose parents had been in our home but were no longer in residence had not finalized payment of their bills. The next two days, Tom was able to collect over $140,000 that had been outstanding. Another miracle of God's grace had taken place, bringing us one step closer to the opportunity to make a difference in our world.

The first phase of the church building was completed in 1969—which included a fellowship hall and gym, several classrooms and kitchen facilities. It was a great day when almost a thousand people lined up in their cars and traveled the seven miles from what was the West Side Gospel Tabernacle to what is now known as Lakeview Christian Center.

The event was not accomplished without some sadness. As construction of our facilities was underway, a young man wanted to start a new church. He went through our congregation and signed up some seventy people to go with him. I had asked the young man to wait until we had our building completed and we would help sponsor the church, but he refused to wait. This was a blow to us financially as our faith was tested one more time. But these times of sifting only caused us to lean on the Lord more heavily, and the Lord proved to be faithful again.

Having gone through a couple of years of real testing, God gave me a song. I knew the Lord had spoken to my heart; I never doubted His guidance, although many times my faith was tested, so I began to sing:

"We've come this far by faith, leaning on the Lord,
Trusting in His mighty hand, He's never failed me yet.
Oh, oh, oh, we can't turn back.
We've come this far by faith."

V

TRAVELING AN UNCHARTED ROAD

Trusting is believing that God will keep His word.
Trusting is believing your ev'ry prayer is heard.
Trusting is letting God know that you're depending on Him.
Trusting is feeling His forgiveness within.
Trusting is believing that God could care for you.
Trusting is believing just as a child would do.
It is like giving your hand to Jesus and knowing He won't let go.

IT was a new day. There was great excitement as our congregation moved to its new facilities located at the cloverleaf of I-465 and Rockville Road. The church was located just two miles from the International Airport. Both the church and the convalescent home were visible to the people of Indianapolis on the interstate that circled the city. God had placed us in a strategic location. We didn't have our sanctuary yet but were able to meet in the fellowship hall.

It was necessary to expand the facilities three times during the next five years as Lakeview Christian Center experienced growth and revival. Growth meant adding new staff, and the addition of staff meant additional expenses. Money was not in abundance in the 1970s. We had incurred enormous indebtedness and overhead expense. In addition to this, occupancy at the convalescent home was not strong enough to carry the overhead from month to month. We found ourselves treading water financially both at the church and the home.

It was a new day, all right. We had embarked on a new road, but were already learning that yesterday's provision is inadequate for today's need. We soon found ourselves running behind, facing another emergency. We needed $100,000 to catch up on bills and stop the bleeding. It was at this time that I was approached by an organization that was moving into the nursing care business. They made an offer to purchase our convalescent home for enough money to pay its mortgage, and that of the church as well. The offer was very tempting and my first reaction was to take it as an answer to prayer. This would have allowed us to finish the sanctuary and concentrate on the church's mission.

It seemed a sensible course to pursue. But in my spirit I did not feel comfortable, and I had walked with the Lord long enough to know that inner voice. After a great deal of prayer, I decided to seek the counsel of others. I called a meeting of seventy-five men of our church, little knowing that that meeting would change the whole course of my ministry.

I laid the whole thing out before the men. I wanted each of them to know the load we were carrying. I provided a detailed financial summary of the church and of the convalescent home. I had gone out on my own with the home, so they weren't particularly interested in that. But when they learned we could the sell the convalescent center and use the money to pay off the church they were ready to go. One after another stood and said, "This is the answer to our prayers. Let's sell the home and free the church of its indebtedness."

Something happened at this moment I'll never forget. The doctor, referred to in an earlier chapter, stood to his feet and asked a very pointed question. Remember, this is a man who was not a Christian at the time, was not a member of our church; he only attended on Easter and Christmas, and perhaps some special event. "Brother Tom," he asked, "did God tell you to build these two buildings?"

This led to a lengthy explanation of what we had done, why we wanted to minister to hurting people in our community. Many elderly folk were not receiving proper care, I told the men, and the church ought to do something about it. I went on for some time, then replied to his question. "Yes," I said, "I believe God planted it in my heart to take this step of faith."

Then the doctor made a statement that forced me to accept the challenge of the Great Commission to "go into all the world and preach the Gospel to every creature" (Mark 16:15). "Then isn't your God big enough to meet your need?"

Now I faced a decision that would alter the road I would

travel from this moment on. With my faith and ministry challenged as never before, it was time for some self-examination. I recalled a promise I had made to God in a very difficult time of building. I told the Lord that if He would help me construct these two facilities, I would raise the finances to build at least one church somewhere in the world every year. Seventy-five men waited for my answer.

I knew I had to say something. After what seemed like an eternity, I looked up and said, "Dr. Hancock, God has helped me to this point, and He is able to meet our need." I reminded the men of the promise I had made and reaffirmed my commitment to obey the Great Commission. I assured them of God's faithfulness and dismissed the meeting. I went home that night with a real peace in my heart and have never looked back.

The next morning I went to my office and called the Foreign Missions Department of the Assemblies of God in Springfield, Missouri. I asked to talk to J. Phillip Hogan, Executive Director of World Missions, and told him what I wanted to do. Is there some place in the world that needs a church, I asked. Some place of primary importance. He told me he had just spoken to two ministers about going to Nassau where there was an urgent need for a church. He asked if I would join them. A few days later, we flew to Nassau.

The Assemblies of God had only one church on the island, a mixed congregation. But there was division between whites and blacks. For years the problem had gone on unresolved. We spoke on a Sunday morning, and after the service told them we wanted to help establish a church for the black community. We were received with great openness by both groups who favored such a move. The next day we went looking for property and located an ideal site. We found the owner and agreed to buy the property. I promised upon my return home to send good faith money and raise the remaining funds within a few weeks.

Back in Indianapolis, the church had turned a corner. It was growing and the finances were increasing. The bank offered us a consolidation loan which took care of our indebtedness and took a lot of pressure off the congregation. But where would the money come from to purchase land and build a church in Nassau? God gave me the idea of creating a bond program that could be sold to business people in Nassau. The Foreign Missions Department would become the holding agency and pay the issue as it came due. I flew back to Nassau and talked to the government agency involved and told them I wanted to raise the money.

They had never heard of such a thing, but were open to it. I contacted several businessmen in Nassau who bought the bonds that were to be repaid with American dollars. Within a matter of weeks, we were ready to build. We sent men from our church to do the building. My responsibility was to complete the construction and raise the money to pay the bond issue as the bonds came due.

God added His blessing and the building was completed. It was soon filled to capacity and two additions were required. Eventually the people were able to build a larger structure that seated over a thousand people. I was privileged to go to Nassau in 1997 and preach the first week of services in their large new building.

Now that we had begun our journey down an uncharted path to "make a difference in our world," it was time to more fully involve our congregation in fulfilling the Great Commission, to remind them of the words of Jesus spoken in that brief period between the resurrection and ascension. It was His last command to the church, so important that each of the Gospel writers record it. The only thing Jesus left in this world was wrapped up in the Great Commission.

I wanted our church to feel the impact of our Lord's words in the last meeting with His followers: "Go ye into all the world and preach the Gospel to every creature" (Mark 16:15). "Go" speaks of action, and the implication is that now is the time to get started: Go now! Whatever else the church may do, it will be marked by barrenness if it is not a "going church."

As pastor, I had the responsibility of instilling this message in the hearts of our entire congregation. Everyone must take this task seriously, the Great Commission was not meant for a few. Our first step in bringing awareness to our church was to set aside a weekend to highlight world missions. We invited Phil Hogan, Executive Director of World Missions to come for the weekend and tell our people how we could get involved in what God was doing in our world. Our church had been giving about $20,000 a year to missions, but on the Sunday night of that weekend pledges totaled $100,000. Over the next few years we set aside one week a year to promote missions, and in a few years our people were giving over a million dollars a year.

Our missions convention became the highlight of the year. Much planning was required to make this a success, so in January I would appoint fourteen couples to form a committee, with each couple responsible for some aspect of the convention scheduled for the first week of October. The committee would decide on a theme for the year and everyone would begin working from that theme. Couples would be responsible for promotion, children's and youth ministry, meals, ushers, music, missions booths and "taste of missions." They would arrange for missionaries to spend an evening in a home. This enabled our people to get acquainted with their families and over a meal to learn something about their field of labor. Everyone worked together, with different people responsible for the missionaries' travel back and forth, meals, and any needs they might have. A member of the committee arranged for missionaries to get into our schools and talk about the country they came from.

Our people were very creative in getting everybody involved. One night there would be a children's service with the auditorium decorated in the motif of some country. Another service would involve the young people. A tent was purchased so the youth could have their own service and at the close of the convention the tent was packaged and shipped to a country to be used for evangelism.

A typical week would involve many activities. The convention started on a Sunday with a parade of flags from fifty-six different nations and missionaries dressed in the costumes of their countries. During the parade pictures of the missionaries and their projects would be shown on a giant screen. When everyone was in place, the choir sang a great missionary song, followed by a keynote message.

On Monday night we would meet for dinner at a hotel in the city. This was a very important event that included the missionary families, the mission's committee and the entire church staff. This was a time to get acquainted, instructions were given to the missionaries and assignments for the committee and staff were made. Members of the staff would be responsible for the missionaries' travel around the city, equipment they might need for their presentations and to assist in any way possible.

During the last two days of the convention missionaries would meet with our staff to share special projects that required necessary funds. Each evening a missionary was assigned to speak to at least two groups of people of the congregation for at least half an hour. A time of fellowship followed each service with a "taste of missions" where at least six different foods from six countries were available to taste. Missionaries would set up booths with literature, films and artifacts from the countries of their calling. Each night after all the activity was over one of the staff members provided a lunch and a time of fellowship for the missionaries and the church ministry staff.

There were a number of different meetings on Saturdays including a men's breakfast and a ladies' brunch. A great banquet was held that evening with the leadership of our church together with the missionaries who had been with us that week. This was a special time of challenge, concluding with prayer for the Sunday services when commitments would be made for the coming year.

On Sunday night the faith promise offering was received and commitments made for the coming year. To the missionaries participating in the convention, an amount of additional support was promised. A special offering was given each missionary, a personal check was given to their families, and a check was provided for their travel expense. The great annual missions conventions were a reminder of why we're here and of the urgency of getting the job done before the night comes.

The words of C.C. Grant express the reason we placed such importance on fulfilling the Great Commission:

> *Seest thou the clock of time,*
> *Its hands now past eleven?*
> *The hour of twelve is drawing nigh,*
> *Then . . . time no more is given.*

Seest thou the harvest fields,
The stalks of grain now whitening?
In the darkened skies the thunder rolls
Amid the flash of lightning.

Look again! The Lord of harvest stands
His head now bowed in reckoning,
The strain of tears in on His face,
His hand to you is beckoning.

Wilt thou take time for pleasures now?
Wilt thou take time for sleeping?
One short hour for you is left,
One short hour for reaping.

Hearest thou those pleading cries?
The souls of men are calling.
At thy feet the sickle lies;
Above you grain is falling.

Work awaits in yonder fields,
There's work for you, O reaper.
Thrust in thy sickle and reap the grain,
The call of souls grows deeper.

VI

MAKING A DIFFERENCE

*Your core values are a reflection
of what you will suffer for.*

Floyd McClung

THE early church dared to do the impossible, to go into all the world with the good news of Christ's plan of redemption. To move across the great Roman world, a pagan empire, with the story of an obscure man who died and rose again and now offered forgiveness of sins and eternal life, made no sense—unless these witnesses had experienced that forgiveness and tasted the powers of the world to come.

And look at them: Simple men and women, farmers, fishermen, a tax collector. Without social, political or ecclesiastical standing. They had no funds and owned no property. They knew nothing of radio, television, printing presses and other tools of propaganda. But they knew God, and they were convinced that Jesus Christ is the Son of the living God through whom one may receive salvation and citizenship in an eternal kingdom.

In his famous wartime book, *They Were Expendable*, Will White records the dramatic story of a squadron of PT boats made of plywood, powered with Packard engines, each manned by twelve men. Not one of the boats sent to the Philippines returned and only four of the seventy-two men survived. White quotes one of the four survivors: "You see, we were expendable."

Paying the price to make a difference is what it takes to fulfill the commission of our Lord. Each of us can make a difference. Each of us can determine to do something meaningful to touch lives, lift burdens and make a change for eternity.

"It is possible to evade a multitude of sorrows by the cultivation of an insignificant life," writes John Henry Jowett, a great English preacher. "If a man's ambition is to avoid the troubles of life, the reason is simple: Shed your ambitions in every direction. Cut the wings of every soaring purpose. Seek a little life with the fewest contacts and relations. If you want to go through the world with the smallest amount of trouble you must reduce yourself to the smallest compass. Small souls can dodge through life; bigger souls will be blocked on every side. As soon as a man begins to enlarge his life, his resistance is multiplied."

Shortly after completing the church in Nassau, a challenge came from a missionary in Calcutta, India. Mark Buntain had gone to Calcutta some twenty-five years prior to the time he spoke for us at Lakeview Christian Center. Calcutta is a city of millions with some of the worst conditions I have ever witnessed anywhere in the world, with hundreds of thousands of people living on the streets. Povertyis everywhere, sickness, disease, hunger and filth. Mark and his wife Hulda brought their great hearts to this city of hurting people and began to minister to their needs.

The Buntains had developed a feeding program where stations around the city offered food to the hungry. I had visited Calcutta and witnessed the scenes that are hard to describe. I watched as they lined up for blocks waiting to receive just enough food to last for the day. Twenty-seven thousand women, boys and girls were fed each day. Mark believed that you could not minister to a man's spiritual needs while he had unmet physical needs. Thousands of churches and organizations across Canada and the United States supported this effort.

If permanent changes were to be made, the children needed an education, so Mark began a school program. It grew until there were 14,000 boys and girls gathering at different places in the city attending classes. Because many of the children came from the streets, they needed suitable clothing, so uniforms were provided. Each morning the boys and girls would pick up their uniform, dress for school, then at the close of the day change back to street clothes.

A clinic was opened for the sick and infirm but that was inadequate to meet the needs, so funds were raised to build a magnificent seven-story hospital right in the heart of the city. The hospital was equipped with the finest doctors and nurses available. The quality of the hospital is reflected in the fact that Mother Teresa reserved a room where she knew she would receive quality care when required.

The spiritual needs of the people were not neglected. Mark Buntain built a church that ministered to people of seven different languages. He raised funds to sponsor other churches in the area. A Bible school continues to train young men and women for ministry.

While Mark was preaching at Lakeview Christian Center in the early 1980s, he asked if we would help sponsor a church in the Dum Dum area of Calcutta at the cost of $85,000. This seemed like a big step for us to take but I was confident God wanted us to move out of our comfort zone and assume responsibility for the building of this church.

My wife, Lois, and I were invited to go to Calcutta to preach under a tent at the property they had purchased for the church. The national pastor already had a small building and had started a school and had one of the feeding stations in his area. Upon arrival at the property the pastor and his wife and some of the teachers had prepared a lunch for us. This was a very interesting experience because I didn't recognize most of the food that was set before us. Then they poured a little orange drink in the glass and filled it up with water. Those standing around the table watched to see if we would eat the food. When I saw Mark eating everything, we entered in and ate along with him. The people were pleased that we did not refuse their offer of hospitality, and we won their hearts. We ministered for four nights to these people who were hungry for the Gospel.

Lakeview Church's missions giving had increased from $20,000 a year to over $250,000. We began sending money to build the new church in India, then upon completion they asked if we would return for the dedication. Hundreds of people were gathered outside this lovely building when we arrived. The pastor wouldn't let anyone inside until we arrived as he wanted us to cut the ribbon and be the first ones inside. The congregation was so thrilled that they began to march around the building. Three times they marched around and sang songs of praise to God. We had now built our second church overseas.

When we returned to Indianapolis and shared the story of our experience in Calcutta, and showed pictures of the building with the hundreds of people gathered together, I knew we were on a course to make a difference in many countries around the world.

Church in Calcutta, India.

It was only a few days after our return from Calcutta in 1974 that I had an unusual experience. I often went for prayer at the prayer chapel at six o'clock in the morning. One morning God began to deal with me concerning a man who was a developer in our city. Roy Prock was not a member of our church, but the Lord brought his name to my mind. I was impressed to go and talk to Roy about his giving. Since he was a member of another church, I wrestled with the Lord about the assignment. I felt it would be improper to talk to him about a need in a church he did not attend, and certainly it was not about any personal need I may have had at the time, so I argued with the Lord.

Finally I gave in. But it was not easy for me, for I had never talked to anyone personally about their giving or about any need. I called Roy on the phone and asked if he could give me five minutes if I came over to his office. He graciously consented and gave me directions to his office.

Before I left my office I picked up several missions brochures that had been sent to me. I picked up three of them, thinking the Lord might want me to talk about missions. Upon arrival at Prock's office, I said, "Roy, I'm here on a very strange assignment. Your name kept coming to me as I was praying. God seemed to be impressing upon me to come and talk to you about your involvement in foreign missions. "

I told Roy that I had not come for any personal reason or on behalf of the church I pastored. "But," I said, "I would like to leave these brochures with you and if God is talking to you, perhaps you'd like to call Springfield, Missouri, and talk with Phil Hogan, Executive Director of our world missions program."

Tears brimmed in Roy's eyes as he related to me how the Lord had been speaking to him. He promised to discuss the matter with his wife, Wanda, and I left his office.

A few days later, Roy Prock came to my office and said, "I understand you are building a Teen Challenge Center here in the city and Wanda and I would like to help." With that he handed me a check for $30,000. "Don't just give me the check," I said, "but make it a matching gift and give me thirty days to raise the other $30,000.

He liked that, and I went to work calling pastors and asking each one for a thousand dollars in order to match the grant. Thirty churches responded and $60,000 was given to build beautiful facilities for Teen Challenge in Indianapolis.

A short time later Roy came to my office and asked if we were going to sponsor another church soon. If we had something in mind he wanted to help. I told Roy that I had been praying about doing something in Argentina. I told him that I had a feeling in my spirit that God was getting ready to do something very special in that country and I wanted to invest in it.

"Let me give you $25,000 for the next project," Roy said, as he handed me a check. I told him I didn't have anything in mind but would call the Foreign Missions Department to see if they had something we would like to be a part of.

I called Springfield and asked to speak to Phil Hogan. He was in an emergency meeting, I was told, and if I would leave my name and number he would get back to me. "Is this important?" the secretary asked.

"Well," I replied, "I have $25,000 that I would like to give for a project in Argentina if there is a need." "Wait a minute, this is important," the secretary said. Within moments Phil Hogan was on the line. "Tom, what's this about $25,000?" he asked.

I told him my story, then he told me his. "We're meeting right now to deal with an opportunity we have in Buenos Aires. Tom," he went on, "we can purchase a building for a church near the heart of the city, valued at $200,000. We can buy this property for $25,000 if we come up with the money by Friday of this week. Loren Triplett is down there now trying to work out something. All we need is $25,000."

"Call Loren and tell him the money is on the way," I said. That night I received a phone call at 11 o'clock from missionary Ralph Hiatt. He was rejoicing, believing that God had performed a miracle. Ralph told me that they had two hundred people gathered under a tent, praying that somehow the Lord would provide $25,000 by the weekend to enable them to buy that property for their church.

Making a difference—that's what it's all about. And now it was happening. A few weeks later Ralph Hiatt called again, told me that they had purchased the building, and wondered if I would come to Buenos Aires and preach at the very first meeting in the new building. I said that I would love to come and celebrate with them, but would it be all right, I asked, if I could bring Roy and Wanda Prock with me since they were the means of the answered prayer.

A few weeks later we were off to Argentina, where a number of unexpected things began to happen. But first we had a great celebration together as we enjoyed the first service in the newly purchased building. Then I was asked to speak at a ministry being held on a street corner. A young Bible school student was conducting services every night on one of the main streets at the entrance to the city subway. He would set up chairs, microphones and instruments and hundreds gathered to hear the music and listen to a message.

This young man, Oswaldo, was given a warehouse where he could hold services if he was able to gather enough people to make it a success. Roy Prock, who was a developer, offered to design the building for him, make a nice entrance, build a balcony and enlarge the facility to accommodate twelve hundred people. We were able to help finance the project, and when we returned several years later, Oswaldo, the young man who started on the street corner, had a congregation of 8,600 members. God had sent revival to the city of Buenos Aires.

We next visited the Bible college which we found to be in great need. The main building demanded immediate attention, the chapel was unfinished, and there was a shortage of housing. Accommodations were limited to sixty or seventy students. We came along beside Rocky Grams, president of the school, and committed to help make improvements, purchase additional property and remodel the buildings. Today the school is producing hundreds of ministers each year who are not only touching Argentina but sending missionaries around the world.

Over the next few years we were able to help three Bible colleges in Argentina and assist with construction of a number of churches. Reports of revival continue to pour in as of this writing. We give all the glory to God for a great harvest, the result of the faithful efforts of many people determined to obey the Great Commission.

As our involvement in South America increased, a special time of God's visitation seemed to be on the way. We were invited to join missionary evangelist Bernard Johnson holding a crusade in Brasilia, Brazil, where we saw thousands come to Christ. It was at this time that Bernard talked to us about a Bible school, children's ministry center and a Bible school extension center he was developing. With such an ambitious program it is no surprise he was short of funds.

He invited us to come to Campinus and see what he was doing. I had already planned a return trip to Argentina and told him I would come to Campinus at that time. Roy and Wanda Prock and another couple, Jim and Sherry Smith, accompanied Lois and me on our return trip to Buenos Aires, then on to Brazil, where we visited the school and the other ministries. The major outreach ministry of the school was supplying material for seventeen thousand ministers in Brazil with twenty-nine college level courses. Ministers gathered in groups all over the country and studied together, and completing a lesson, they would send it to the office in Campinus for grading. A second lesson would be sent and so on until the twenty-nine Bible courses were finished. Thousands were being equipped in this way to be more effective ministers of the Gospel. At the completion of their studies they came to Campinus for intensive review before graduation.

This seemed to be an ingenious way to equip ministers, and we agreed it ought to continue. We learned it would take $450,000 to finish the facilities and they could not continue building unless the money was there. We made arrangements to provide the money, borrowing the biggest part of it.

What a thrill it has been to know that you are participating in the training of young men and women who are carrying out the work of the Gospel. Making a difference is what it is all about and we challenged our people to get in step, assuring them that one day they would witness the results of their obedience to the Great Commission.

Literature center in Campinus, Brazil.

We faced another opportunity when we were invited to Quito, Ecuador. Our missionaries, Paul and Lana Duda, were in need of securing property and asked us to survey the situation and see if we could help. The ministry under Pastor Cabraero was being held in a rented four-story office building in a downtown area. Services were being held on the first floor, a clinic was functioning on the second and a day care on the third and fourth floors. The building could be purchased, but we weren't certain it would be adequate for long.

Around the corner we found an abandoned theatre that would accommodate at least eight hundred people. We offered $465,000 for the theatre and for the building they were renting. The properties were owned by five different families, and bringing them together was not an easy task. Just when we thought we had a deal, one of the families backed out.

I made a quick trip to Quito and told the owners that if we didn't finalize the purchase within three hours we were going to look elsewhere. That helped them clarify their minds. We purchased the property, renovated the theatre and were privileged to once again attend the dedication of another lighthouse established for the glory of God.

Our efforts in South America were just getting started when we were invited to speak at the Bible college in Barquistmento, Venezuela. The seven buildings on the campus were about forty years old and urgently in need of modernization. The superintendent of the Assemblies of God of Venezuela wanted to bulldoze the entire campus and conduct classes in different churches while new buildings were being constructed. We suggested they not interrupt the school but replace the buildings one at a time as they carried on the work. David Wagner, missionary contractor, was called in on the job, and over the next several years saw the entire campus rebuilt, which included a large meeting place to accommodate special gatherings of the churches of Venezuela.

Teams from many churches across the United States flew down and worked on the buildings. Seventy-five pastors from Venezuela would take off a day each week to work on the campus. Hundreds of ministers are being trained each year at this location, which is a testimony to the faithfulness of God. Other victories were recorded in Peru and Columbia and elsewhere across South America.

Bible college, Barquistmento, Venezuela. Two of the seven buildings.

We were able to finance some eighty different projects around the world during my last years as pastor of Lakeview Church. As my seventieth birthday approached, I sensed something in my spirit suggesting a change in the direction of my life. I had served five different churches over a period of fifty years, thirty-eight of those as pastor of my home church in Indianapolis, the church my parents served for twenty-five years. All but twelve years of my life had been spent here, and the roots were deep.

During the first part of 1994 I called the church to a week of prayer. The Lord was doing some special things in our church at that time. Toward the end of that week of prayer, God spoke to my heart and said it's time to release the responsibility of the church. I had two sons who were pastoring in the same city and I felt this would give me more time to spend with them in their ministries. I made my intentions known to our church and appointed a search committee to begin looking for my successor. I decided to take a couple of weeks and go to Florida and endeavor to find direction for my life. It was there God gave me an expanded vision for missions around the world.

HAVE ANY BEEN MISSED?

Suddenly, before my inward, open vision
Millions of faces crowded up to view.
Sad eyes that said, for us is no provision;
Give us your Savior too.

Give us, they cry, your cup of consolation,
Never to our outstretched hands is passed;
We long for the DESIRE of every nation,
And, oh, we die so fast

Does He not love us too, this gracious Master?
This from your hand alone we can receive.
The bounty of His grace; oh, send it faster
That we may take and believe.

VII

WHEN BARRIERS CRUMBLE

You have nothing to do but to save souls. Therefore spend and be spent in this work.

John Wesley

TEAR down this wall!" Ronald Reagan implored General Secretary Gorbachev, as he addressed the thousands gathered at the Brandenburg Gate in West Berlin June 12, 1987. "If you seek peace," the American president said, "Come here to this gate! Mr. Gorbachev, tear down this wall!"

The Berlin Wall, known in the Soviet Union as the "Anti-Fascist Protective Rampart," a separation barrier between West Berlin and East Germany, had sealed the border between East and West Berlin for twenty-eight years. Construction on the wall, which began in 1961, not only stopped the flow of those fleeing Communism but also closed the door for carrying out the Great Commission in that part of the world, an extension of Communism's aim to stamp out religion altogether.

But "the word of God is not bound" (2 Timothy 2:9); bricks and mortar are no match for the sovereign God. A chain of events began to unfold in 1989 that witnessed the collapse of the "death strip," the Berlin Wall, ushering in a new day of opportunity for the Gospel.

A number of years before, Lois and I had been invited to speak at a conference in West Berlin and at a United States army camp in Heidelberg. While there, a couple of soldiers asked if we would like to visit East Berlin and offered to take us over for a glimpse behind the Iron Curtain.

We crowded into a small Volkswagen and crossed into East Berlin at Check point Charlie. Our first impression was that we had just entered a third world country. The streets were void of cars, the stores empty of goods and people. Up a back street and through an alleyway we were taken to a room where believers met to worship. You could tell they were conscious of being watched. We felt great oppression just visiting for a few hours with people who had been stripped of all liberties.

Robert Mackish, a missionary friend of ours, invited us to come to Bratislava, Czechoslovakia, in the fall of 1989. This was just two weeks after the wall had come down. We invited Charles Crank, superintendent of the Assemblies of God in Indiana, and his wife, Jan, to accompany us on the trip. We spent three days with the leaders of a group called the Pentecostal Union. This was the first time these men had been together in twenty-eight years. Doors were beginning to open for the Gospel and they were looking for direction and support. We heard testimonies of men of God, some of whom had spent as much as twenty-five years in prison for preaching. We discovered that there were thousands of Christians in country after country who had been faithful through great trial.

We helped them form a fellowship that would enable them to keep in touch with each other and learn from each other as to how best to take advantage of the new opportunities that lay before them. I felt I wanted to do something to assist in a special way and believed that the answer lay in establishing Bible schools and colleges designed to prepare a new generation to spread the Gospel message. Jesus said, "Go and make disciples of all nations, baptizing them in the name of the Father and of the Son and of the Holy Spirit, teaching them . . ." (Matthew 28:19, 20).

"One of the fundamental reasons for the failure of the church to implement the last command of the Lord Jesus Christ is the lack of the right structures," writes Patrick Johnstone. I felt unworthy being in the presence of these men and was determined to do something meaningful for the harvest. Over the next two or three years we observed what was happening. Many came from the West to take advantage of the new opportunities to preach the Gospel, but sadly, the majority came for personal publicity, enthralled with the crowds, returning home with pictures and glowing reports, but leaving little behind. Who would establish these people in the things of God? Who would provide training for these faithful men and women now sharing Christ in a once-forbidding land? This is where we pledged to make a difference.

When we left Bratislava, we flew into Moscow and stayed at the Intercontinental Hotel just off Red Square. We met the bishop of the Pentecostal Union and promised to help purchase a place for the training of leaders. We found a building we could purchase for $200,000. When the doors were opened, young people came eager to learn. It was my privilege to address the first graduating class of fifty-seven. Many of these students established churches, became pastors and presidents of Bible schools throughout the old Soviet Union.

We returned to Moscow two years after the school opened, arriving on Easter Sunday and were thrilled to see huge signs posted that read, "He is risen . . . Christ is alive."

We were able to rent community cultural centers seating eight hundred people for ten dollars a week and sponsor a pastor for a whole year for a thousand dollars. When we told our congregation what so little money could accomplish, many responded to help mother a church. The harvest was white and ready to be reaped.

We flew next to Kiev, Ukraine, where we had been asked to help raise money to purchase a building for a Bible college. A suitable building had been located and could be bought for $17,000. We immediately sent the money and secured a property worth half a million dollars. The government had just released properties back to their original owners, many of whom had no money and could do nothing with them, making it possible to take advantage of the situation.

Bible college in Kiev, Ukraine. ActioNow purchased this building soon after the fall of the Berlin Wall, enabling nationals to carry the Gospel to their own people.

Four thousand churches of the Pentecostal Union are led by pastors who received their training at this Bible college. Again I was invited to speak at the first graduating class with some forty students receiving degrees, and to think $17,000 is all it took to make a difference in that part of the world!

At a world missions fund-raising meeting, some of the field directors asked if we would visit the Bible college in Minsk, Belarus, where they were witnessing a special move of the Holy Spirit. We were able to raise sufficient funds to erect a building adjacent to a church which had a regular attendance of four thousand people. Young people were willing and ready to enter the harvest and needed training. We did some teaching in the classrooms, then spoke at the first graduation.

I constantly remind donors that participate in this worldwide ministry that eternity will reveal the fruit of their sacrifice. In their giving, they are laying up treasure in Heaven as men and women come to know Christ. I recall an old song my parents used to sing, and have sung it to groups of dear friends who have labored with us:

They come from the East and West,
They come from the lands afar,
To feast with the King, to dine as His guest,
How blessed these pilgrims are.
Behold His hallo'd face
Aglow with light divine,
Bless'd partakers of His grace
As gems in His crown to shine.

I'll look on the great white throne
Before it the ransom'd stand,
No longer are tears, no sorrow is known,
Nor death in that goodly land.
My Savior has gone before
Preparing the way for me.
Soon we'll meet to part no more
Thru time and eternity.

The gates of that holy place
Stand open by night and day.
O, look to the Lord who giveth more grace
Who alone has prepar'd the way.
A home in those mansions far
His hand hath reserv'd for all.
For the wedding feast prepare,
Obeying the gracious call.

O, Jesus is coming soon, the judgment will then begin.
O, what if our Lord, this moment should come
For those who are free from sin.
O, then would it bring you joy or sorrow and deep despair
When the Lord in glory comes, we'll meet Him in the air.

The most moving service I had ever experienced in any of these schools occurred at the Silk Road Bible College in Bishkek, Kyrgyzstan. God helped us raise the funds for the college and I was asked to speak for the first graduating class of 37. These students had endured great persecution, with threats of prison, even death. When I asked what these young men and women would be doing after graduation, I was told they would be starting churches or filling in for pastors who were in prison, some of them facing possible execution. These young people were ready to pay any price to go with the Gospel.

There was a special eagerness about this first graduating class. I'll never forget four young ladies who upon graduation decided to start a church. They were the first women to dare to preach or pastor a congregation in the country of Kyrgyzstan.

Silk Road Bible college, Bishkek, Kyrgyzstan.

The bishop of that area was present for the graduation and related a story of God's providential care. He was the pastor of a church in Uzbekistan with 4,500 members. He was stopped on the highway one day by a group of men who had been sent to get rid of him. As the men pulled out knives and guns he said, "Before you kill me, grant me one request." He asked to be allowed to pray. He knelt in the street and began to call out to God. Conviction seized the would-be executioners, and the longer he prayed, the heavier the conviction grew. The next thing the bishop knew, the men were on their knees giving their hearts to the Lord.

ActioNow had previously purchased a large warehouse for this pastor and had it remodeled for a place of worship. It provided room for 5,000 people. This church had reached out to other communities and started over a hundred new churches.

Roy and Wanda Prock traveled with us on this trip as well as Jerry Parsley, field director for Euro/Asia Missions. We left Bishkek with great satisfaction, knowing that we had been able to make an investment in the college, and seeing the fruit of that investment. From Bishkek we flew back to Kiev in the Ukraine to visit the Bible college and to assess progress on the building of a theological seminary in which ActioNow had made an investment.

The Ukraine government had given property to the Pentecostal Union large enough to build a church and a seminary. Finances had been raised by the Pentecostal Union, Mission of Mercy, ActioNow and others to begin construction, but now the money had run out bringing the work to a halt. It was at this time that a special miracle took place.

One of the couples with us on the trip asked me if I thought the project was worthwhile, and what it would cost to complete the building. I explained to them that the Bible college would train leadership for the fifteen states of the old Soviet Union and their churches. The seminary would provide the necessary degrees to make them acceptable to the government. The couple made a commitment to finish the building. It was my privilege to speak at the opening of the facility and also serve on the board along with the bishops representing the fifteen states of CIS (Commonwealth of Independent States).

Ribbon cutting, Theological seminary, Kiev, Ukraine.

In 2002, Lois and I, Sam and Joyce Johnson, Jim McNabb, a pastor from Oklahoma, along with the field director for the area were invited to go to Tiblisi, Georgia. The ministers of the area had requested help in developing a Bible school. Revival had come, churches had sprung up, but there was an urgent need for a training center for the pastors. A church in Oklahoma had already advanced $50,000 to purchase the land for the building.

Upon arrival, we were taken to a piece of property we decided to purchase, together with additional land which would provide better access. We met with local architects who designed a building with an estimated cost of $750,000. After lengthy discussion and prayer we decided it was possible to undertake the project. The three of us, McNabb, Johnson and myself, made a commitment to raise $250,000 each to underwrite the building of the Bible school.

When he arrived back in the United States, Sam Johnson contacted twelve pastors and invited them to go with him to Tiblisi, Georgia. He would show them the property and ask the pastors if their churches would raise $25,000 each toward the project. Upon arrival in Tiblisi, they went to look at the site, unaware that a defrocked priest had pledged to stop the building of the Bible school. A hundred angry men accosted the pastors, assaulted some of them, and took their cameras, watches and other valuables.

One of the missionaries had a cell phone with which he called the police who rescued the pastors, took them to their hotel, stood guard until the next morning and escorted them to the airport. Before they left for the United States, Sam Johnson called me and told me what had happened. Immediately I put in a call to our senator from Indiana, Richard Lugar, who was chairman of the Foreign Relations Committee. The Senate had just released $800,000 in aid to the Republic of Georgia so I knew the senator had some connections with the officials of that country. Sen. Lugar made a call and assured me that the government would take action.

The defrocked priest had stirred up his followers and invaded other churches and meeting places, destroying property and assaulting worshipers. The government arrested and imprisoned the priest and warned him not to interfere with our people.

Out of all of this the government called and told us of a four-story building that was available for less money than we had planned to spend on the original site. The building was purchased and remodeled with an auditorium that seats 500. The remaining floors were remodeled for offices, classrooms and dormitory area for the students. So we ended up with a much larger building than the one we had first wanted, at a savings of $250,000. What the enemy meant for evil, God meant for good (Genesis 50:20).

A couple of years ago, we invited our missionary in Siberia to fly to Naples, Florida, for the annual ActioNow board meeting, to share with us what God was doing in that far-off land. When he told us his school had been holding classes in a one-room rented facility with no assurance that they could rent it from one month to the next, we made a decision. ActioNow pledged $345,000, and with help from some others, they were able to dedicate the Siberia Bible School in October of 2006.

As the wall that separated countries began to fall, spiritual barriers that enslaved human souls began to crumble as the people of God began to make a difference in the old Soviet Union.

Siberia Bible College, Omsk, Siberia. ActioNow provided most of the funds for construction of the college, dedicated October 16, 2006.

This chapter is dedicated to the twenty church leaders of the Commonwealth of Independent States to whom we promised our help in building Bible schools and colleges. With God's help, we have been able to establish eight Bible schools and a theological seminary that have trained and equipped hundreds of men and women to be effective leaders, pastors, teachers and soul winners.

VIII

ACTION 2000

The program of your life should be His and not your own. World evangelization is God's program for His people in this age. It must be our highest priority and financial responsibility.

LAKEVIEW Church's missions endeavor was becoming stronger every year. Our people had caught the vision and our conventions were becoming more inspiring every year. In preparation for the convention in 1988, one of our men approached me with an idea and a challenge.

"I believe there are people God has blessed in some special way," he said, "who would like to have more of a hands-on involvement in missions. Think of what could be accomplished if they were challenged to increase their participation, and felt they had a part in making the decisions that determined the projects chosen and funds expended." He went on to suggest I give some thought to this and come up with a plan to make it more personal.

After a few days of thought and prayer, an idea was born in my heart of reaching out and organizing a group of individuals to take on priority missions projects. I went back to the man who had made the suggestion and asked if he knew of a businessman whom he thought would share our vision. He gave me the name of a man in Lafayette, Indiana. The idea sounded great to him and he offered the name of a man in Rockford, Illinois, who might be interested. I called him and told him what we had in mind, of how we could make a greater impact in the world by working together.

The idea was catching fire. This would be the origin of ActioNow, the name ultimately chosen for this organization, referred to in earlier chapters. I reached a businessman in Colorado who was not only interested, but invited us to meet at his vacation home in the mountains to work out the details. We set a date to meet and invited Phil Hogan, Executive Director of our worldwide missionary enterprise, and his assistant, to attend the organizational meeting. The three days in the mountains were a very productive time during which we agreed on some broad principles. For one thing, we wanted projects that could be completed within the year they were funded. By having a report on either a finished project or one that was nearly finished would inspire the donors when they gathered for their annual meetings.

It was very important to us to have accountability. Phil Hogan set up a special account with the Foreign Missions Department. Donors could send money to our account that was accessible on a day's notice. Springfield would keep the books, send receipts to the donors and give local churches missions credit. Since 1988, this plan has functioned very efficiently and we have been able to work without delays.

We decided to meet twice a year with the field directors representing South America, Africa, Euro/Asia and the Asia Pacific nations (two additional directors have since been added for China and Western Europe). The directors would screen the projects, determining which were of priority. A priority project was one that required immediate attention to provide growth and/or a place to train national leadership. Was this need urgent, essential to the effectiveness of the ministry on the field without delay? Those were the questions. The purpose and principles of Action 2000 (now ActioNow) were settled. Again, we would commit to projects that were urgently needed and that would be finished or nearly finished by the time we met again. This has been accomplished each year.

We left Breckinridge, Colorado, feeling that we had accomplished something meaningful for the Kingdom of God. We decided to meet the next the year in Phoenix, Arizona. We met twice a year over the next three years and raised over a million and half dollars allocated to some eighteen different projects. We began to reach people who had a heart for missions and wanted to know what their investments were doing. The more they knew, the more likely they were to increase their participation from year to year.

The World Missions Department began to think in similar terms. Why not promote a program nationwide that raised millions of additional dollars in addition to what the churches were doing? They came up with the idea of organizing what they called a "Fly-In." Lay people and pastors from across the country would come together and be challenged with opportunities they could support.

The first Fly-In was held in Dallas, Texas in 1991. It was well attended, but the amount of money raised was disappointing. Lacking was the personal touch that made people feel they were part of something significant. It seemed like an extension of the local church program already involved in missions.

The Action 2000 group felt they should disband their effort and join the national group to show their support. Over the next three years very little money was raised for priority missions projects at the Fly-Ins, which seemed to be more of a promotional tool than a fund-raising instrument.

Shortly after resigning from the Lakeview Church, my wife and I received a call from Loren Triplett, the new Executive Director of World Missions. Triplett felt that our group had been very successful in raising funds and wondered if we had ever thought of reestablishing the group that made up Action 2000. I told them that Roy Prock and I had talked about it, so the call was confirmation that we were on the right track. We sat down and began to plan a meeting for the latter part of 1994. Wanting a more central location in the United States, we settled on Springfield, Missouri, the headquarters of our missions department, which graciously hosted a banquet for the gathering.

About fifty people attended the meeting, several from the missions department, several pastors and a number of lay people from different parts of the country, all of them excited at the prospect of doing something special for the Kingdom of God. We agreed that we were not interested in redirecting money already coming in through the churches, but wanted to raise new funds. We soon discovered that the pastors had their own agenda and any monies they would commit had already been designated for missions. Although they applauded our efforts, it was something over and above what they were doing, so we began to concentrate our efforts with business people and other lay folk who would step forward and go the extra mile.

We planned to meet once instead of twice a year because it seemed difficult for some to take off and travel halfway across the country too frequently. Action 2000 became the theme as we began our journey toward the turn of the new century. We were grateful that the Lord had helped us reestablish a relationship with old friends and find new ones who would help us pay the debt we owed a weary world. The words of the apostle Paul reminded us of that obligation: "I am debtor both to the Greeks and to the barbarians, both to the wise and to the unwise. So as much as is in me, I am ready to preach the Gospel . . . (Romans 1:14, 15).

There are seven reasons why every believer ought to be personally involved in missions. I would like to share with you why ActioNow embraces these reasons as we journey together through the next six years.

First of all, it is sinful not to share one's blessings with those less fortunate. This obligation is illustrated in a story found in II Kings chapter seven. Four leprous men, outcasts, are dying for lack of food. Perhaps the Arameans, camped nearby, would give them something to eat—or they may kill them; after all, they are lepers, outcasts.

"We're destined to die one way or the other," they

concluded. "Why sit we hear until we die?" Although they didn't know it, the Lord had caused the Arameans to hear the sound of chariots and horses and a great army, and had abandoned camp, and when the lepers entered, they found food and drink, and silver and gold. It was then they were reminded of their families back home without food or drink. "This is a day of good news," they said, "and we remain silent. If we wait until morning light, some punishment will come upon us. Now therefore, come, let us go and tell the king's household."

They felt they had no choice but to share what they had found. One is reminded of Jim Elliot, who wrote to his parents of his intention to take the Gospel to the Indians of Ecuador. When friends suggested he might be more effective in this country, where many know so little of the Bible, he replied: "I dare not stay home while Quichuas perish."

Secondly, it is sinful to disobey the clear command of our Lord. Jesus commanded His followers: "Go ye into all the world and preach the Gospel to every creature." The Great Commission was the most far-reaching and demanding command Jesus ever gave. Our primary reason for existence is to take the Gospel to a lost world. The word "go" is a choice word our Lord used in the New Testament:

Jesus said to the ten lepers who were healed, Go!

Jesus said to the blind man at Jericho, Go!

Jesus said to the woman with the issue of blood, Go!

Jesus said to the delivered demoniac of Gadara, Go!

To each of us who have been set free, He says, Go!

People the world over desperately need the life-saving message of salvation, a third reason for missions. Through Jesus Christ, men and women can find a way out of poverty, ignorance and injustice. Jesus taught men and women to deal justly with each other, and with mercy, just as He showed mercy. The Gospel can solve the most difficult problems.

A fourth reason for the necessity of missions has to do with the eternal destiny of men. There is a life to come, and preparation must be made. Building hospitals and schools and clinics does not absolve us of the responsibility to warn the wicked to prepare for eternity. "Knowing the terror of the Lord," Paul said, "we persuade men" (2 Corinthians 5:11).

A fifth reason ActioNow is compelled to come alongside our missionaries with every possible assistance is because there is no other way to be saved if Jesus Christ is not preached. Jesus said, "I am the way, the truth, and the life. No ones comes to Father except through me'" (John 14:6).

Modern man dismisses the unpleasant subject, but there is a hell at the end of a Christless life, and the sixth reason we labor in the vineyard is to remind men and women that judgment awaits us all after death.

The seventh reason missions exists is that there is no other way to be obedient . Every Christian must be a missionary or help send one, or make provision for those who go. Why missions? Because God, our conscience and the world's urgent need demand that each of us do his best to share the story of Christ with everyone. "To be a missionary," someone has said, "you don't have to go around the world, you just have to go outside yourself."

Here is what happens when people dare to move outside themselves. In 1994, a small group gathered in Springfield, Missouri, ready to combine their efforts in advancing the cause for which Christ came into the world. Six projects were chosen from the many presented, and our people sprang into action. Our group pledged $40,000 for a Bible school in Cameroon, Africa. The second project represented the first step into Communist China, where we were able to locate and purchase a place to train believers. Then two purposes were served with the purchase of a church and a Bible school in Ranchi, Bihar, India, with an investment of $40,000.

Church and Bible school, Ranchi, India.

Earlier I had been invited to speak at a ministers' seminar in Bucharest, Romania, where I was introduced to a Romanian pastor who was starting a Bible school. Along with the missionaries there, we saw the need for a training center and pledged $250,000 to purchase a building for the fledgling school that has now trained hundreds of young people who are preaching the Gospel in that country. Over the year, the original building was outgrown and five and a half acres were purchased for expansion. On that property today is a campus, one building with an auditorium seating seven hundred, fourteen classrooms, six offices and the largest theological library in Eastern Europe. The second building houses eighty- four students plus a modern kitchen and dining room, all debt free!

Action 2000 was not finished investing in 1994. We accepted a challenge to match a $100,000 gift for a Bible school in Andhra Pradesh, India, so $200,000 was made available to purchase a suitable site, large enough to begin construction on the school.

The sixth project of that year was in Latin America, where we were able to assist with the construction of a training center in Suriname, formerly a territory of the Netherlands, now a republic on the northeastern coast of South America. Total investments in priority missions projects for that year were $661,484.25.

Rejoicing abounded as the group gathered in Springfield in 1995 to review the achievements of the previous year from China to Latin America. Nine new opportunities were presented and Action 2000 responded. They included a Bible school in Madagascar; a church in Congo, Africa; a radio station in Adidjan, Ivory Coast; a church in Indonesia; a lecture hall in Jaotong University in China; a Bible school in Guayaquil, Ecuador; a Bible school in Cordoba, Argentina; a church in Arequipa, Peru; and a down payment on property for a Bible school in Bishkek, Kyrgyzstan. Three hundred and fifteen thousand dollars was raised to meet the needs in these nine areas of the world.

Again in 1996 nine projects were presented and Action 2000 was ready to help. The total raised that year was $336,000 for a Bible school dormitory in Angola; a building for the West Africa School of Theology; property for a church in Niger, Africa; the Happy Horizon Children's Home in Cebu, Philippines; a school for tribal children in Laos; additional funds for the Bible school in Kyrgyzstan; help for the Bible Institute in Panama; a Teen Challenge Center in Costa Rica; and a building in Costa Rica for language training for missionaries going to Central and South America.

In 1997, Action 2000 held its meeting in Orlando, Florida. We rejoiced as the field directors reported on the victories achieved the previous year. A special report on what was happening around the world was provided by the Executive Director of World Missions. Seven new projects were presented for consideration: Cape College of Theology; Cape College of Theology Grad Center; Mozambique Training Center; Ministry Center in Thailand; and a special project in Albania, a country once totally atheistic where missionaries were not even allowed to enter the country. Gospel tracts had been handed to people through fences and God began to do something significant among the people. The Lord opened a door for us to build a school building in Albania that doubled for a church, the first one in that country.

Cordon Christian Center in Uruguay and a Bible college in Minsk, Belarus, were the two final projects to which we committed funds that year, bringing our total investment in 1997 to $430,500.

When the group comprising Action 2000 met in 1998, with the year 2000 approaching, some thought a better name might be fitting, one more suited to the challenges of the twenty-first century. After a number of suggestions were considered, we coined a word, ActioNow, thus retaining our identification with the past, "action," and expressing our determination to do the work of Christ "now."

It is so easy to procrastinate. Put it off. Wait until retirement to get involved in the Sunday School. Teach a class of boys and girls sometime, but for one reason or another it doesn't get done. We were determined not to make that mistake. We would proceed without delay to undertake the work to which we had been called. With a deep conviction that God had called us at a strategic time to accomplish big tasks we reaffirmed our commitment to the mission with a new name, ActioNow.

Ten opportunities were presented in 1998, some needing help finishing construction from previous years, others were new adventures and there were some major projects that would go on for a number of years. Mission of Mercy requested $60,000 to match a gift of that amount needed to get started on the Evangelical Theological Seminary in Kiev, Ukraine. ActioNow had already purchased a building for a Bible college, but now that there were several schools and colleges throughout the old Soviet Union (now known as CIS), there was a need for advanced training for leaders of these schools, and leadership for the growing fellowship of believers as hundreds of churches were being started in many of the countries.

Evangel Theological Seminary, Kiev, Ukraine. ActioNow provided over $800,000 for construction of building which serves both the church and seminary, for training of leadership in the fifteen states of CIS.

A real miracle took place when the government gave us a piece of property in Kiev to build both a seminary and church in the same building. The property has high visibility, located in the heart of the city. Our contribution of $120,000 enabled them to begin construction. ActioNow contributed to nine other projects in 1998: help with construction of a Bible school in Patagonia, Argentina; a Christian worship center in Uruguay; a school in West Africa; a ministry center in Chad, Africa; an evangelistic training center in the Philippines; assistance with a Bible school in Greece; a kitchen and dining room at Mount Hope College in Lisbon, Portugal; a Bible school in Venezuela; and a tent seating five thousand for Hosanna Worship Center in Managua, Nicaragua. ActioNow committed $361,725 to assist these endeavors.

God was not finished working miracles—for which we were grateful. To keep everything in perspective, we were not a large group, seldom with more than fifty attending our annual meetings. Now we were heading into the last year of a decade and of a century, facing enormous challenges. As we met in 1999, the field directors were ready. There was always more to do. We settled on nine projects. We promised to help the Esther Center in the Ivory Coast, a training center for young girls; a primary school in Equatorial Guinea; an orphanage in Kenya, West Africa; a worship center in Addis Ababa, Ethiopia; a church building in Tashkent, Uzbekistan large enough for five thousand worshipers; an evangelistic training center in Rome; a Bible college in Barquistmento, Venezeula; Nicaragua Family Worship Center; and Evangel Theological Seminary in Kiev, Ukraine.

One of 7 buildings of Barquistmanto, Venezuala Bible School.

The miracle is that God provided the funds to meet all of these ministry opportunities, totaling $1,183,143. We had begun to see what God could do with even a small group as they dedicated themselves to make a difference. Only eternity will reveal how many thousands of people have been touched by the message of hope and love because of the obedience of the people of God. What a wonderful time awaits them when they hear the Master say, "Well done, good and faithful servant."

"He who has no vision of eternity will never get a true hold of time," observed the Scottish writer Thomas Carlyle. The best time-management technique I know is to live in the light of eternity. Contemplation of three future events will help frame what we do in this vapor called time. They will occur as surely as tomorrow's sunrise.

The first event is the Judgment Seat of Christ. The apostle Paul describes it in 2 Corinthians 5:10, 11: "For we must all appear before the judgment seat of Christ, that each one may receive the things done in the body, according to what he has done, whether good or bad. Knowing, therefore, the terror of the Lord, we persuade men." This is the judgment of the believer.

The second event is the Great White Throne Judgment. This is the judgment of unbelievers from all the ages. John describes the terrible scene in Revelation 20:11, 12, and 15: "Then I saw a great white throne and Him who was seated on it. Earth and sky fled from his presence, and there was no place for them. And I saw the dead, great and small, standing before the throne, and books were opened. Another book was opened, which is the book of life. The dead were judged according to what they had done as recorded in the books . . . . If anyone's name was not found written in the book of life, he was thrown into the lake of fire."

The third event is the gathering of the Company of the Redeemed. In chapters five and seven of Revelation, the apostle John sees a company of the redeemed of all ages pouring out praise to the Lord. "After these things I looked, and behold, a great multitude which no one could number, of all nations, tribes, peoples and tongues standing before the throne and before the Lamb, clothed with white robes, with palm branches in their hands, and crying out with a loud voice, saying, 'Salvation belongs to our God who sits on the throne, and to the Lamb.'"

This is Mission Accomplished!

IX

THE TWENTY FIRST CENTURY

He who has no vision of eternity will never get a true hold on time.

Thomas Carlyle

HE calendar announced a new year, A.D. 2000 (*anno Domini, "in the year of our Lord"*), but this was more than another new year. We stood on the threshold of a new decade, a new century and a new millennium. Two thousand years ago our Lord gave us a great commission. How were we doing?

It was my custom at the beginning of a new year to take inventory of my relationship with the Lord and my service to Christ. I prayerfully sought guidance as to the goals we should pursue to further the Kingdom of God. But this year seemed to be an especially challenging time with a sense of urgency permeating my thoughts and prayers. There were a number of reasons for the intrusion of this sense of urgency in my spirit.

The march of prophecy was at once thrilling and unsettling. The signs of the times pointed unerringly toward a conclusion of some kind. The late J. Phillip Hogan, who provided dynamic leadership of world missions for the Assemblies of God for so many years, once said, "As the nations, one by one, pile up their baggage of cultural stresses, politics and war, and head on down the road toward Armageddon and the twilight of the church age, their steps seem to quicken."

We live in a global world that is shrinking, when it is easier than ever to reach the nations of the world. We live in a time when modern communication makes it possible to get the message to every nation. We live in a society that has the means to finish the task.

The first reason for this sense of urgency in my soul was a consciousness of the lateness of the hour prophetically. But there was another reason. After preaching the Gospel for more than six decades, at the age of seventy-six, I was aware of the hands on the clock. Each of us is given a window of opportunity. No one knows when that window will close. Even our Lord was conscious of this sense of time, "I must work the works of him that sent me while it is day," He said, "before the night comes when no one can work" (John 9:4).

The Son of God redeemed the world with great difficulty, so none of us is exempt from the assignment, or the sacrifice involved in fulfilling the commission. God has so much confidence in the least of us that we have the honor of being a last-lap runner. We are in a race, a relay; others have blazed a trail before us and the baton has been handed down to us. It is the task of the last runner of the relay to reach the goal. Too many are depending upon us. We shall not fail!

God in His mercy gave me favor with a small group of like-minded lay people who believe as I do, that if we join our efforts together, we can provide funds for priority missions projects, funds that were not being raised through normal channels. It is nothing short of miraculous that a group, never numbering more than thirty-five or forty people, has over the last few years raised over $13 million . What a thrill it has been for Lois and me to travel the world and witness what God is accomplishing through His people.

A few years ago I attended the graduation of one of my sons and heard the speaker, who was the head of a department of education, say, "In the 1960s, we settled for being second-best in America. We opted for more coffee breaks and worried less about being number one, or producing the best. We chose to be more relaxed, to enjoy the good life." Then the speaker listed the results:

We do not have the best steel.

We do not produce the best clothes.

We do not produce the best electronics.

We do not produce the best automobiles.

The twenty-first century demands our best. Here's what

the apostle Paul opted for, "We are constantly ambitious, and strive earnestly to be well-pleasing to Him, for we must all appear before the judgment seat of Christ" (2 Corinthians 5:9, 10, New Authorized Version). Look at the words: "ambitious," "strive," "well-pleasing." That's what it takes to be a winner.

We are not content to *run* in the race; we are determined to *win*, and winning demands an all-out effort. It suggests excellence in performance. Excellence is the result of honest effort, a by-product of character. It has nothing to do with setting records, winning awards or acquiring fame or fortune. It has everything to do with selling out to Jesus Christ and making His cause your own, with no consideration of the cost. Howard Hendricks, longtime professor at the Dallas Theological Seminary, said, "Talk is cheap, dedication is costly."

During the 1984 Olympics, a little teenager named Mary Lou Retton won the hearts of the American people. She captured the gold medal in the women's all-around gymnastics competition, and won two silver and two bronze medals in team and individual events. She scored a perfect 10 in the vault event, and she became the first American to win five medals in gymnastics.

What made Mary Lou a winner? It was simple—but not easy. She practiced five hours a day, six days a week, and her coach said she was always ready to go. When asked to do some extra work, she would say, "Let's go!"

The prophet Daniel gives us the secret of how to make a difference in a culture foreign to our own: "The people that do know their God shall be strong, and do exploits" (Daniel 11:32). In the New Testament, the apostle Paul echoed the spirit of Daniel, "As much as is in me, I am ready. . ." (Romans 1:15); and "I press toward the mark for the prize . . ." (Philippians 3:14).

Remember when the nation of Israel faced extinction when they were captives in Persia? Haman, mortal enemy of the Jews, had devised a plan to destroy them. Working within the law, they would all be killed if they disobeyed the king's order. Xerxes, the king himself, was unaware of what was happening. Esther's uncle, Mordecai got wind of the plot and challenged his niece to intercede: "If you keep silent, at a time like this," he warned Esther, "deliverance and relief will arise from some other place. God has placed you in a position to avert a disaster. If you fumble the opportunity to interdict the intentions of evil men, your life is in jeopardy, along with your people." Then Mordecai utters this great sentence: "Yet who knows whether you have come to the kingdom for such a time as this?" (Esther 4:14).

Esther responded to the urgent appeal, and directed her uncle to mobilize the people and call a fast. "If I perish, I perish," she cried, and set in motion a series of events that overthrew the enemy and saved her nation. Total commitment made her a winner, and total commitment will speed us on our way toward total obedience to the command of Christ. "We cannot be responsible for the next generation," Billy Graham once said, "but this is your day, this is your generation. We can fail, or we can choose to make a difference."

ActioNow is gripped by this same sense of responsibility, motivated by a love for Christ and people for whom He died, and driven by the awareness that the time is as short as the need is great. We believe that the priority of training nationals is of utmost importance. They are the ones best equipped to reach their own people. They are in place, they know the culture and they speak the language. Our job is to provide the tools, give support and back them in our prayers.

I want to close this chapter with a sentence I read somewhere: "You can make a difference in our world. Never settle to just get through, or get by, but rise to the challenge of our day. When the world is at it worst, we need a people that will be at their best."

Pat Williams, Executive Vice President of the Orlando Magics, wrote a book entitled, *Who Wants to be a Champion?* In this book he gives ten building blocks on how to make a difference in the world:

- Think the right kind of thoughts
- Say the right kind of words
- Set specific goals
- Take responsibility for your actions
- Choose the right kind of friends
- Turn failure into strengths
- Go the extra mile
- Never give up
- Remember that character counts
- Live by the faith phenomenon

Receiving Christ as your personal Savior is not where the adventure ends. That's just the beginning of the most amazing, incredible and exciting life one could ever imagine. So I urge you to dedicate your life, get involved, make yourself a better person and the world a better place. Cling to God's hand at all times. Do what you can to touch your world. Hearing the words, "Well done," will make it all worthwhile.

AD 2000
AND A TASK UNFINISHED

"Jesus is Lord—Lord of the past, of the present, of the future. Jesus is Lord of everything. Jesus is Lord, unqualified. So until the kingdoms of this world become the Kingdom of our Lord and Christ, until this gospel of the Kingdom is preached in all the world for a witness, until every last creature has had an option to say what he will do with Jesus, let us tell the world that Jesus has already given us the victory. Let us go forward in His name!"

E Stanley Jones,
missionary to India for sixty years

WO thousand years ago, Jesus gave us the Great Commission. Two thousand years later, the task remains unfinished—and time is running out. That's why the last week of January 2000 found us once again gathering for prayer, discussion, planning and action. There were forty of us who met in Indianapolis to lay the groundwork for another great year. Loren Triplett, Executive Director of World Missions, led in a time of devotion, then summoned us to once again engage the battle.

Reports then were given on nine projects completed the previous year, some in particular that were outstanding. For example, the building we purchased in Tashkent, Uzbekistan, was overflowing with a congregation of thousands. The first of nine buildings on the campus of the Bible college in Barquistmento, Venezuela, had been completed. Lois and I had the privilege of going and speaking at the graduation held in the first new building. While we were there, about forty ministers came with their sledge hammers and tore down one of the old buildings. There was great excitement among the nationals as they began to see the campus being rebuilt with more adequate facilities.

In 1998 ActioNow had purchased a tent for a meeting place in Managua, Nicaragua. The congregation had grown to several hundred and a permanent building was needed. Our oldest son, Tommy, had started a church on the north side of Indianapolis and watched it grow in numbers and expand its facilities, until it occupied eighty-one acres and a magnificent sanctuary in a prime location.

Tommy had a heart for missions, and wanted to adopt a country and come alongside the leadership of the churches and make a difference. Under his leadership, his church built orphanages, churches, homes for the needy and a school for the deaf. In the midst of such victories, in the prime of his life, our son fell ill with ALS, or Lou Gehrig disease, and in January of 1999, Tommy went to be with the Lord.

The leadership of our churches in Nicaragua called and asked if I would sponsor a project to honor our son who had done so much for that country over the past seventeen years. We decided to build a worship center on a piece of property overlooking the city. ActioNow hired a local architect to draw plans for a building that would seat eight hundred people, at a projected cost of $1.2 million.

David Wagner, missionary contractor, and I studied the plans to see how we might better spend the money. We discovered that by using different material and redesigning the plans, we could have an auditorium accommodating twenty-five-hundred people. We also added a lower area for Sunday School classrooms and training rooms.

When we went looking for a local construction superintendent to oversee the project, we found a twenty-eight-year-old lady who could manage it for us. It was a wonderful arrangement with David or myself flying down once every other month to check on progress and deal with any problems that had arisen. When the building was completed, the total cost came to $865,000. God had crafted another miracle.

Twenty-five hundred people crowded into the building, with another thousand meeting under a tent. Over four hundred responded to dedicate their lives to Christ on that memorable day.

Our son's entire family attended the opening service that day as the new worship center was dedicated in honor of Tommy Paino, given in loving appreciation for his service to the people of Nicaragua.

As I write, six thousand souls gather on a given Sunday to worship the Lord. Three services are required to accommodate the crowds that throng the worship center. That's what happens when a handful of people work together to touch lives. This is the reason ActioNow is in the soul winning business, impacting lives for eternity.

Hosanna Worship Center, Managua, Nicaragua. ActioNow provided funding and oversight in building this 2,500-seat auditorium where 6,000 worshipers gather weekly.

Other ministries ActioNow invested in during the year 2000 were: a church in Eritrea, Africa; a Bible school dormitory in Madagascar; Saminaka School in Nigeria; a medical storage facility in Cambodia; Battle Front Hospital in Mongolia; Romania Bible School; Bogota Bible Institute; Managua Worship Center; and Tiblisi, Georgia Bible College.

In 2001, ActioNow met again in Indianapolis, especially interested in a report from Tiblisi, Georgia, where a number of pastors who had gone with Sam Johnson on a fact-finding trip had been assaulted by an angry defrocked priest and his gang. God turned things around, and out of that disaster came a smashing victory. We learn again and again that we must not be frustrated by circumstances, but always possess an abiding confidence in God and deep sense of mission.

From its birth in the Upper Room, the church was destined to be an aggressive, militant movement possessing spiritual authority, bringing a message of redemption and healing to hurting people everywhere. Before His ascension, our Lord commissioned His followers with a mission and a message. "Whenever you enter a town and they receive you," He said in Luke chapter ten, "eat what is set before you; heal the sick in it and say to them, the Kingdom of God has come near to you."

When the seventy He had sent out returned, and reported, "Even the demons are subject to us in Your name," Jesus replied, "I saw Satan fall like lightning from heaven!" What was Jesus telling them: "Why shouldn't you see people set free? I saw Satan defeated. I was there, when he was cast out of heaven."

So we have the authority to go. We have been given a mission and a message with credentials and motivation. What hinders us from finishing the job?

Almost $700,000 was pledged in 2002, and I was amazed and pleased to report that ninety-eight percent of all money that has been committed has come in over the years. It is also important to note that no money has ever been used for office expense, travel or salaries. One hundred percent of every dollar has gone to make possible a priority missions project.

ActioNow made nine different projects a reality in 2002 including dormitory, dining hall and kitchen at the Bethel Bible College in Manila, Philippines; a Bible college in Siberia; expansion of the university in Bucharest, Romania (of which more details later); a Bible college in Myanmar; and support for Builders' International, a team which oversees construction projects around the world.

Bethel Bible College, Manila, Philippines, dormitory, dining hall and kitchen.

The Bible school in Siberia brought to eight the number of Bible schools or seminaries ActioNow has sponsored in what was once the Soviet Union, that great union of countries which covered fifteen percent of the land mass of the earth. Hundreds of trained workers are scattering out across this once-darkened mass of humanity. As Noah, moved with fear, built an ark to provide salvation for all who would accept; as Moses served his generation, "choosing rather to suffer affliction with the people of God than to enjoy the pleasure of sin for a season," so a tightly-knit group of businessmen have pooled their efforts and resources to assist those who carry the Gospel far and wide.

The gifted and dedicated Henrietta Mears, Christian educator, author and speaker, once said, "God will not leave us alone when we labor beyond our strength to do His will." We are not alone in this business. We have the abiding presence of the Lord, and we labor in the succession of giants: Wycliffe, Huss, Calvin, Luther, the Wesleys, George Whitefield, Finney, Moody, and in our day, Billy Graham. And the call still rings out for laborers who will redeem the time. None of us has the promise of another day. The command to go with the Gospel supersedes all other orders, and the call comes from One who transcends all other voices.

"Only one life, t'will soon be past,
Only what's done for Christ will last."

The story is told of a veteran missionary couple returning home after a lifetime of missionary service, facing the diseases and heat of Africa. They happened to be on the same ship on which Theodore Roosevelt was returning from a big game hunt. Crowds with blaring bands, colorful banners and a host of celebrities welcomed the president.

The two faithful pioneers of the Gospel descended the gangplank carrying an old cardboard suitcase. Observing the great ovations heaped upon Roosevelt, the little missionary lady looked at her husband, with his well-worn clothes, weathered features and his yellowing pith helmet, and said, "Daddy, we are coming home after forty years in Africa and there is no one to meet us. He spent a few weeks on a big game and comes home to a great ovation." Whereupon the intrepid pioneer took his wife's hand, and said, "Mother, don't worry, we're not home yet."

Our God not only inhabits eternity; He inhabits infinity. Jesus said, "In my Father's house are many mansions . . . I go to prepare a place for you" (John 14:3). One of these days, when the last tyrant has risen and fallen, when civilization has jerked to its last convulsion, and the Lord God has brought this age to a fiery end, you and I will stand on the hill of Zion and shout Hallelujah! For the Lord God omnipotent reigneth, King of kinds and Lord of lords, and we shall reign with Him forever and ever!

There is a final majesty in this mission. Let us neither slumber nor cease until the Master of the harvest writes across the Great Commission—Finished!

Can we, whose souls are lighted
With wisdom from on high;
Can we to men benighted
The lamp of life deny?
Salvation, O, Salvation!
The joyful sound proclaim,
Till earth's remotest nation
Has learnt Messiah's name.

-Reginald Heber

XI

WORK AWAITS IN YONDER FIELDS

Give me the love that leads the way,
The faith that nothing can dismay,
The hope no disappointments tire,
The passion that will burn like fire.
Let me not sink to be a clod,
Make me Thy fuel, Flame of God.

Amy Carmichael

I F we dare answer the call to enter the whitened harvest fields, we will encounter difficulties; but we shouldn't be surprised. Why, then, pursue a task so fraught with challenges? First of all, do we have a choice? A sense of *debt* compels us. The apostle Paul exposed one of the great driving forces of his life when he said, "I am a debtor" (Romans 1:14). Charles Finney, used of God to bring revival to America, declared, "I am gripped by the responsibility I have to men and women everywhere.

If duty demands we enter the harvest, a sense of *devotion* keeps us there. "The love of Christ constrains us," Paul wrote (2 Corinthians 5:14). Christ's love for us and our love for Him thrusts us into the harvest. Why get involved in missions? We are obligated, we are debtors; and the love of Christ moves us, that's devotion. There's another word, *duty*. Winston Churchill understood that word. At the height of the Second World War, he warned his countrymen, "We must do more than our best, we must do what is required." Paul said, "Necessity is laid upon me, yes, woe is me if I do not preach the gospel" (1 Corinthians 9:16).

World evangelism becomes an integrating theme around which all other concerns revolve. A sense of *direction* in world missions not only benefits the people we reach with the Gospel, but serves as a cohesive function in the life of the one who goes with the good news. Paul said, "I was not disobedient to the heavenly vision" (Acts 26:19). The final reason for obeying the call flows out of a sense of *destiny*. Think of it, we have the privilege of helping set the timetable for the end of the age.

With these compelling reasons behind us, who can shirk the responsibility? None of us are exempt from the commission or the sacrifices that commission entails. We have a story to tell, a message to fallen man. It is the story of a birth in Bethlehem, a thorn-crowned brow in Jerusalem, a cross just outside the city walls and an empty tomb that changed the course of history forever.

The Subject of the story, Jesus Christ, after the victory of the cross and the resurrection, returned to the Father. But before ascending, He gave the charge, "Go into all the world." That is the reason the men and women who are a part of ActioNow are willing, and eager, to make the personal sacrifices required to let all men know that God loves them.

And so we came together in 2003, once again to receive some thrilling reports, and to explore new opportunities. It was another year, and the task remained unfinished, so we were ready when twelve new projects, which included the Polish Bible School in Warsaw; a ministers' training center in Spain; Africa Hope Literature Center; Cochabama Bible School in Bolivia; a church in Tanzania; a television station transmitter in Brazil; City of Refuge in Jamaica; an addition to the deaf school in Nicaragua; Managua Worship Center, a chapel at Beijing Theological Seminary; Bucharest Bible College and Builders International. Over $850,000 was committed in 2003 to spreading the Gospel and training workers. From east to west and from north to south, lives are being touched because someone gave.

In 2004, Sam Johnson partnered with us in raising money for priority missions projects. His coming on board was a great asset as he was still active in preaching in our churches across the country. ActioNow's main source of income was lay people who wanted to do something special over and above what their churches were doing, and to participate in projects that could be completed from year to year. Many of these people traveled with us to the far corners of the earth to see what they were accomplishing; to Russia, South America, China, the Philippines and Europe.

Sam's emphasis was raising funds through the churches, enlisting the personal help and support of pastors, so together we enlarged our borders and set out on a course to do more than we had done in the past. Someone said, "No one discovers new lands without consenting to lose sight of the shore for a very long time." In 2004, ActioNow was ready to take that plunge, and that year we raised $1.3 million.

One of the most exciting things that took place was a trip to Armenia, a small land-locked nation that for decades had been closed to the outside world. Only twenty percent of the people have jobs, and the others have learned to live off the land, and share with each other. But the amazing thing is that revival came to Armenia and the people needed help. We undertook to raise money to either build or purchase buildings, and/or remodel existing facilities to provide places for worship. We were able to take on thirty churches during the year 2004. A number of pastors had the opportunity to go to Armenia on a special Sunday set aside to dedicate the buildings. They returned with tears of rejoicing to tell their congregations what God was doing in that little country, where the powers of darkness had reigned so long. We had pictures of each of the buildings made available to the churches.

Africa's Hope Literature Resource Center requested additional help. A large building in Springfield, Missouri, had been built for the purpose of distributing literature to the many nations of Africa. But by developing a more central location, distribution could be made more quickly and more efficiently.

Another exciting project was the construction of a Bible school in Kinshasa, Congo, a nation which had been devastated by terrorists over the past ten years, but was now exploding with revival and church planting.

Kinshasa School

Other projects sponsored in 2004 were Bethel Bible College in Manila (completion of a building); a church in Loilio, Philippines, also additional money for the Bible school in Myanmar; an extension on the International Correspondence Institute; purchase of literature for distribution throughout Asia; a Bible school in Tashkent, Uzbekistan; Xianing Christian Church, Zhao Xian Church and Harbin Bible College in China; additional funding for Managua Worship Center; Tiblisi, Georgia Bible School; and the Bucharest Bible University.

When he saw the smoke rising from a thousand African villages where the name of Jesus had never been heard, Robert Moffat, one of the early missionary pioneers, cried with great emotion, "We shall have all eternity in which to celebrate our victories, but we have only one swift hour before sunset to win them!"

Our Lord said it in these words, "I must work the works of Him who sent me while it is day; the night is coming when no one can work" (John 9:4).

The year 2005 proved to be a banner year in giving, with $1.6 million committed to nineteen different projects around the world. ActioNow pledged the balance needed to finish the Siberia Bible College, except for furnishing and equipment provided the following year. A Bible school in Algeria was started; $270,000 was given to West Africa Theological Seminary to build a library; $100,000 was given for the Caribbean Retreat Center; and $100,000 was designated for the Christian Family Worship Center in Buenos Aires.

Other ministries we supported included Brussels Theological Seminary; Nepal Bible College; Tajikistan Retreat Center; additional assistance for the Polish Bible College in Warsaw; Mayanmar Bible College, Uzbekistan; Builders International; Honduras Worship Center; Belarus Bible College; and the Bethel Bible College in Manila.

The first building of the Bible college in Pointe Noire, Congo, was completed. This is located in the Republic of Congo. There is also a Democratic Republic of Congo where another Bible school has been made possible by ActioNow.

Bible college, Pointe Noire, Republic of Congo. Dormitory, kitchen, dining hall and girls' training center.

Albania was experiencing spiritual growth, and churches were being established in this country, newly-opened to the Gospel. When asked for assistance in building a Bible college, we joined in with Sam Johnson, who had organized "Priority One," a group of pastors and lay people who had gotten involved in special projects. Plans were drawn and a contractor hired. Cost was to be about $750,000. We were able to raise $250,000 in 2005 to get construction going. The building was completed and a service of dedication was held in September of 2007.

The apostle Paul never lost the wonder of the Damascus Road experience, where he had that heavenly vision. He often recounted the events of that day in his preaching, as he did when he stood before King Agrippa (recorded in Acts 26:29). A question we might ask ourselves is: How clear is our vision?

To complete the task of world evangelization, three elements mentioned earlier are imperative, and worth repeating, because without them we'll never get the job done. They are vision, mission and resources.

A vision of the cross is necessary to understand the urgency and magnitude of the task before us. When the awesomeness of that vision fades from our minds, we are certain to fail in our mission. The far-famed Baptist preacher, Robert G. Lee, described the cross as the place "where the history of human guilt culminates. It is at the cross where the purposes of divine love are made intelligible. It is at the cross where our condemnation is lifted, the world is stripped of its charm, the bitters of life are sweetened and the serpent's head is bruised. It is at the cross the darkness of eternity is irradiated and the fountain of salvation is unsealed."

The mystery of our mission is that through the cross, men and women are saved.

"What makes life dreary is the want of motive," George Eliot once observed. Unless human service is motivated by divine love, it will fall far short of either success or satisfying the heart of God. What motivated the apostle Peter to stand unafraid before the murderers of Christ on the Day of Pentecost and call them to repentance? It was the love of Christ. What sustained Paul when he was scourged at Philippi and stoned at Lystra? What motivated Luther to defy ecclesiastical, civil and military despots arrayed against him at the Diet of Worms? What motivated John Knox to rebuke Mary, Queen of Scotland, or made John Bunyan willing to spend twelve years in Bedford Jail, rather than betray Christ? What impelled Adoniram Judson to face cruelty in Burma? Why would five young men leave their families and risk their lives to take the Gospel to the Indians of Ecuador?

Hype, manipulation, ingenious programs are inferior motivations when one is facing the loss of all things, persecution, even death. There is no greater incentive than that of divine love – Christ's love, shed abroad in our hearts. That's the only explanation for the unceasing efforts of ActioNow. The measure of God's love is expounded in John 3:16: "God so loved the world that He gave His only begotten Son, that whoever believes on Him should not perish but have everlasting life." The measure of our love is demonstrated by our obedience to the Great Commission.

Sacrificial giving is the approach God took in supplying the resources necessary to save the world. It can be no different for us. The principle of sacrificial giving is expressed in 2 Corinthians where Paul says, "For you know the grace of our Lord Jesus Christ, that though He was rich, yet for your sakes He became poor, that you through His poverty might become rich."

To provide salvation cost the Father His Son, and it cost the Son His very life. Can we do less than give our all, everything, to follow the Master?

With truths like these driving us, our people set a new record. In 2006, $1.9 million was given by ActioNow and Priority One, including a dormitory for the Bible school in Pointe Noire, Congo; Theological Seminary Extension School in Kanshasa, Congo; a training center at Pamplona, Spain; finished the Bible school in Poland; built two duplexes for faculty at the Asia/Pacific Theological Seminary at Baguio, Philippines; Honduras Worship Center; Thailand Bible College; a printing press for International Correspondence in Manila, Philippines; a Bible school in Botswana, Africa; Philippines Bible College; finished the dormitory, dining hall and kitchen at Bethel Bible College in Manila; Algeria Bible College; finished the Siberia Bible College; Tonga Bible School; Albania Bible School, which was dedicated in September 2007; Davao Family Circus, a wonderful children's ministry; and the Brussels Continental Theological Seminary.

Albania Bible School

This was a great year. The number of souls reached during 2006 is not known, and all of the results cannot be measured until we get to Heaven, but one glimpse of the face of our Lord Jesus Christ will make every effort worthwhile.

Let me digress just a moment and go back and walk you through one of the major undertakings of our group. The story begins in 1994 when Otis Keener and I were invited to go to Bucharest, Romania, to conduct a week of training for about two hundred ministers. While there, we were asked to come and see the Bible school Dr. Ceuta had just started. Struck by the need to train the young people, without any financial backing, and relying solely on the Lord to provide, Dr. Ceuta rented a four-story building and had about fifty students. Because of the economic condition of the country at that time, students paid no tuition and very little for room and board.

A number of missionaries had been invited to visit the fledgling school, and while we sat around talking, Dr. Ceuta said, "What we need is a board to come along and help us develop this school." He went on to ask each of us to serve on the proposed board. After a lengthy discussion, it was decided to move in that direction. When it came time to appoint a chairman, everyone pointed their fingers at me. I laid down some guidelines, things I expected to happen both with our involvement with the board and with Dr. Ceuta.

I pledged to help raise monthly support, but the students would be responsible for ten percent of their tuition. The local leadership thought this was impossible because the average family income at that time was about twenty dollars a week. I insisted that if their education was to be of value to them, they would have to find a way to participate. I believed that the students needed to learn that nothing is free, and that exercising their faith while in school would make them better pastors and leaders later.

The building was in need of a lot of repairs, so I suggested we look into purchasing the building so we could renovate it. That would be quite impossible, we were told. If it became available, it would cost half a million dollars, but we insisted on looking into the possibility of purchasing the building.

We were in the second year of the school and had raised

$200,000 toward purchase of the building when a miracle occurred. Dr. Ceuta called, telling me that the landlord had decided to sell. The second miracle had to do with the price, when the owner offered to accept $50,000.

We had the balance of the $200,000 we had raised, so we had something to start with for remodeling. We put in all new plumbing and new electrical wiring. We replaced the floor and all the doors and painted both inside and out. Sam Johnson came on the board with us and together we raised enough money to complete the remodeling.

Original Bible college building, Bucharest, Romania.

Several years later it was determined that the school was inadequate for the growth they were enjoying, and additional room was required. I asked Sam to chair a meeting of the board when I had to leave early. The agenda included looking at a piece of downtown property on five acres of land with two large buildings. One building had been used as a garage to house large trucks, the other was used as a storage unit with a landing dock across the entire side of the building.

I received a call from Sam telling me that the property could be bought for $419,000. He wanted to know if there was some way I could come up with the money. I called a lending institution that knew I was involved in missions. They agreed to loan the money at three and a half percent.

Chalk up one more miracle, because it is impossible to find land in downtown Bucharest.

We looked at the large building trying to decide what to do with it. We settled on a plan to tear off the roof and siding outside and all the partitions inside, leaving us with the steel frame of the building. Plans were drawn for an auditorium seating seven hundred; fourteen classrooms, a large library and lobby area, and six offices.

The work began, and Sam and I took the job of raising the money month by month to keep construction going and the project moving forward. As the same time, I was covering the monthly payments on the loan.

Finally, time came for a great celebration as the first building was finished. The only problem was that we didn't have rooms for the students to stay on campus. Consequently, the students had to stay in the original building across the city and ride the train to school every day. We promised the students that by next year we would have a dormitory for them.

We took one more look at this huge warehouse and again drew up plans to remodel it, making room for both a girls' and boys' dormitory, We removed the loading ramp, redid the outside of the building, gutted the inside and made room for eighty-four students, plus rooms for visiting professors, bathrooms, a large dining hall and a modern stainless steel kitchen.

We needed another miracle, because the land and the two buildings had cost right at $2 million. It was time to put the original building up for sale, and God helped us sell it for $865,000. So half the cost of the Bible college in Bucharest was covered by the sale of that building. Sam Johnson and I raised the balance of the money through churches and ActioNow.

Seventy people met in Naples, Florida, for the 2007 meeting of ActioNow. Our world missions director, John Bueno, brought a stirring message from the missionaries, then we heard from the field directors. These are men who carry a heavy burden, with huge responsibility for up to four hundred and fifty missionaries. Once again, over $1 million was raised to make possible the following priority projects: additional money to finish the West Africa Theological Seminary Extension School, which is located in Kinshasa, Congo; a Bible school at Kisangani, East Congo; Global School of Theology Northwest; Cameroon Bible School; money to complete the Bible college in Uzbekistan; purchase of property in Moldova; funds to complete the Bible college in Thailand; Jianqxi Student Center, China; Yan'An Church in China; Continental Theological Seminary in Brussels; International Media Ministries building located in Spain; additional help for the Bible college in Cebu, Philippines and a resource center, including library, offices, etc., for the Asia/Pacific Theological Seminary.

New Bible Univeristy, Bucharest, Romania

David Shibling writes, "The whole world is watching hoping to see a 'global, liberal, evangelical, charismatic radicalism that rejects the lure of sin and refuses to be jaundiced by the world's current condition. The unbelieving wish to see among the believing a brave new church of clear-headed worshipers who envision God's glory drenching every people and nation."

The vision that energizes the men and women whose story is told in this book is expressed in Isaiah 11:9: "They will neither harm nor destroy on all my holy mountain, for the earth will be full of the knowledge of the Lord as the waters cover the sea."

XII

TOUCHING OUR WORLD

*Let my heart be broken with the things that break
the heart of God.*

Bob Pierce

A CENTURY ago a battered battalion of weary soldiers was being pushed back toward imminent defeat. With men falling on every side, the general ordered the bugler to sound the retreat. But there was no bugler; he had just been killed. Anxiously the general inquired if anyone could blow the bugle. One young recruit responded that he could. "Well, sound the retreat," the general ordered. "Sir," the new bugler responded, "I don't know how to blow the retreat. I only know how to blow the charge."

"Then blow the charge!" And with the blowing of the charge the troops were energized, the tide was turned and victory rose out of sure defeat.

Some may think the circumstances call for retreat, but the Master says, "Go!" The Holy Spirit commands us to advance. And the time is now. There must be a sense of urgency in carrying out the Great Commission. This sense of urgency arises out of a clear and unmistakable recognition that to live without Christ is to die without hope. Let the words of the first Pentecostal preacher ring in our ears: "Nor is there salvation in any other; for there is no other name under heaven given among men whereby we must be saved" (Acts 4:12).

The apostle Paul, once an enemy of the cross, was so certain he must go to "the regions beyond," so driven was he by his love for Christ and for a lost world, that his enemies rebuked him, "You've lost it, Paul, much learning has made you mad."

But how can it be otherwise? "Nothing quite so contradicts evangelism as indifference to the lostness of mankind," writes Robert E. Coleman, professor of evangelism at Trinity Divinity School. How can we call for retreat when the task assigned the church two thousand years ago remains unfinished?

When you understand the value of the soul, our mission becomes compelling. When Jesus looked on the multitude, he was moved with compassion. The soul is invaluable; the very breath of God in every man and woman. Nothing is more valuable than the human soul. "What shall it profit a man if he gains the whole world, and loses his own soul? Or what will a man give in exchange for his soul?" (Matthews 16:26).

It is for the soul of man that the great war rages. It is for the soul that Jesus was born, was crucified and rose again. It is for the soul the Bible was given and preserved. For the soul the Holy Spirit broods over the face of the earth. It is for the souls of men and women that believers are empowered by the Holy Spirit to be witnesses. The soul is of infinite value. The most familiar verse in the Bible says, "For God so loved the world that He gave His only begotten Son, that whoever believes on Him should not perish, but have everlasting life" (John 3:16).

This is the passion that gave birth to ActioNow, men and women coming together to accept without reservation the assignment Jesus gave to go everywhere spreading the Gospel. No trip was too far, no expense too great, no suffering too intense, no sacrifice too deep if it meant the salvation of one person for whom our Lord shed His blood.

John Henry Jowett, in his book *A Passion for Souls* said, "The gospel of a broken heart demands the ministry of a bleeding heart . . . We can never heal needs that we do not feel."

Who can contemplate with ease the plight of the lost? Perhaps our trouble is that we don't believe men are lost; we don't "feel" it. Or in our busyness, preoccupied with immediate sensual gratification, we simply ignore it. Martin Marty, eminent church historian at the University of Chicago, has keenly observed that "the passing of hell from modern consciousness is one of the major, if still undocumented major trends of our time."

There are many things I could have done with my life. I could have built bigger barns, accumulated more toys, lived in a finer home, found more time for relaxation and pleasure. But when I saw the hungry and hurting, the lost, shuffling through life facing a Christless eternity, I made a choice.

General William Booth, who gave us the Salvation Army, said,

"While women weep, as they do, I'll fight.
While little children go hungry, I'll fight.
While there is a drunkard left,
While there is a poor lost girl on the streets,
While there remains one dark soul without the light of God, I'll fight."

As a young man I made a choice to "fight to the very end." I gave my life to Christ and offered myself to the Lord to go anywhere He called. I was always interested in missions but didn't feel called to a particular country. So in the providence of God we poured that energy into building a great missionary church, which led ultimately to the ministry we have written about in this book: ActioNow.

None of us have invested our lives in a single country as so many of our wonderful missionaries have. But we have made a commitment to speed them on their way, to help with the purchase of property and construction of buildings, and to provide leadership, counsel and encouragement along the way.

During the Second World War, Winston Churchill set out to "win with words" over Hitler by raising the morale of the nation. Not only did he visit troops and factories, but he went to the out-of-the-way coal mining towns. During one visit to the hard-working coal miners, the prime minister urged them to see their significance in the total effort for victory.

"We will be victorious," he told them. "We will preserve our freedom. And years from now when our freedom is secure and peace returns, your children and your children's children will come and they will say to you, 'What did you do to win freedom in that great war?' Someone will say, 'I marched with the Eighth Army.' And someone else will say, 'I guided the ships that moved the troops and the supplies.' And still another will say, 'I doctored the wounds of those that were wounded.'"

Then the great statesman paused. The dirty-faced miners sat in silence and awe, waiting for him to proceed. "They will come to you," he shouted, "and you will say, with equal right and equal pride, 'I cut the coal! I cut the coal that fueled the ships that moved the supplies! That's what I did! I cut the coal!'"

That's what we have tried to do—"cut the coal." To pay the bills we have developed land, sold real estate, moved merchandise, built restaurants and managed portfolios, but our primary purpose has been, and continues to be, to support the front-line troops. That is our vision and that is our dream.

Bob Pearce, who founded World Vision, came home from war-torn Korea in the 1950s and startled comfortable Americans with a question: "How can we sleep when half the world goes to bed hungry every night?" The task is great, the hour is late; the world's dark night is hastening on. "Our age is but the falling of a leaf, a dropping tear; life is brief and sin is here." How shall they hear without a preacher, and how shall they preach unless they are sent?

Missions is the proclamation of the Gospel to the ends of the earth. It is God speaking through us to let the world know that Christ alone is the answer to the sin and suffering of Adam's fallen race. May it be said of us that when the world was at its worst, we were at our best.

Hear your commission, O church of the Master;
Friends and disciples of Jesus take heed.
How are you doing the work of the Father?
How are you caring for the hungry and needy?

Go to the sheep that scattered and fainting,
Having no shepherds, and tell them to come;
Go to the highways and tell every creature
Still the feast waiteth and yet there is room.

Go, the time shortens, the night is approaching,
Harvest is whit'ning and reapers are few.
Somewhere, perhaps, in the darkness are dying
Souls that might enter the Kingdom with you.

Go, Church of Christ, for He goeth before you,
And all the way that ye take He doth know.
On the bright morrow He'll say, "Come you blessed,"
But till the dawning the message is still . . . Go!

TO BE CONTINUED

The story of ActioNow is not finished. Other chapters remain to be written as God opens the hearts of people to journey with us. You can get further information from Tom Paino: 553 Melark Drive, Carmel, Indiana 46032. Phone: 317.408.7250. Or visit our web site: actionowmissions.org.

APPENDIX

Quotes gleaned from the notes of Thomas Paino, Jr.

"They each had the same *commission* you and I have: 'Go into all the world and preach the gospel to every creature' (Mark 16:15).

"They all had the same *message* we do: 'For God so loved the world that He gave His only begotten Son, that whoever believes in Him should never perish but have everlasting life' (John 3:16).

"Their *motivation* was the same as ours: 'Beloved, if God so loved us, we also ought to love one another' (1 John 4:11).

"They had the same *enablement* as we have: 'But you shall receive power when the Holy Spirit has come upon you' (Acts 1:8).

"They had the same *accountability* to God that we have: 'Let a man so consider us, as servants of Christ, and stewards of the mysteries of God' (1 Corinthians 4:1)."

• • •

A missionary society, deeply impressed with the courageous devotion of David Livingstone, wrote the pioneer missionary, who had paved the way for the spread of Christianity on the continent of Africa: "Have you found a good road to where you are? If so, we want to send other men to join you."

Livingstone responded, "If you have men who will come only if there is a good road, I don't want them. I want men who will come if there is no road at all."

• • •

"The reason missions is important is because people who do not hear about Jesus and have no opportunity to receive Him as Savior, are lost for time and eternity."

• • •

"The Great Commission was the farthest reaching and most demanding command Jesus ever gave His followers during His earthly ministry. The primary reason for the existence of the church is to help people find Jesus as personal Lord and Savior. Jesus is our example of total devotion and consistent lifestyle committed to evangelism. He expects nothing less from His followers."

• • •

"As the Father has sent Me, I also send you" (John 20:21).

• • •

Years ago, Dr. Paul S. Rees wrote this: "The church is not to be a settlement, but a pilgrimage; not an estate, but an embassy, not a mansion but a mission."

• • •

Hudson Taylor, upon returning from China, speaking at a conference, told the story of some Chinese fishermen who allowed a man to drown because his wife could not pay them sufficient money to rescue him. Taylor paused until the indignation of the audience was apparent, then asked, "Is the body of so much more value than the soul? We condemn those fishermen because they could easily have saved the man and did not do so. But what of the millions we leave to perish, and that eternally? What of the plain command, 'Go ye into all the world, and preach the gospel to every creature'?"

• • •

Thomas Zimmerman made this statement: "If we take the Great Commission seriously, we will disregard creature comforts and dedicate ourselves to the salvation of dying souls."

• • •

Patrick Johnstone declared, "My absolute conviction from all research and gathering of information is that we are running the finishing straight of the marathon for world evangelization."

• • •

Mincaye was a member of the spear-wielding Huarorani killing party who massacred Jim Elliot, Nate Saint and three other gallant missionaries in 1955. Today, Steve Saint, Nate's son, lives with his family among the Huaoranis. Mincaye is now an elder in the Huaorani church. And the man who killed Steve's dad is now referred to as grandfather. Only the grace of God can accomplish something like this.

Before thousands of evangelists at Amsterdam 2000, Mincaye gave this testimony: "When I kllled Steve's father, I didn't know better. No one told us that you had come to show us God's trail. My heart was black and sick in sin, but I heard that God sent His own Son, His blood dripping and dripping. He washed my heart clean. Now I see you God-followers from all over the world, I see well my brothers and sisters that God's blood has washed your hearts, too. Go speak about God all over the world. Let's take many with us to God's place in heaven."

"Those five missionaries all had loaded weapons with them; guns that, in that moment of horror and glory, they chose not to use. You can counter aggression with reprisals. You can counter rhetoric with rhetoric. You can counter bombs with bombs. But aggressive love, how do you counter that?"

• • •

"Missions is not the ultimate goal of the church, worship is. Worship is ultimate because God is ultimate, not man. Missions is important because the goal and aim is to bring nations to the place of worship, to give glory to God."

At the end of the nineteenth century two French writers went to visit the well-known French scientist, Pierre Bethelot, a kind of scientific prophet. He forecast some of the weapons of mass destruction which would appear in the next century. "We have only begun to list the alphabet of destruction," he told the writers. Silence fell over the meeting. Then the elder of the two writers said quietly, "I think before that time comes, God will come down like a great gatekeeper with His keys dangling at His waist, and say, 'Gentlemen, it's closing time.'"

As we look at our world, it's just about closing time. Our Lord tied together two great themes: world evangelization and the climax of history. He said, "This gospel of the kingdom will be preached in all the world as a testimony to all nations, and then the end will come."

• • •

"If you want to know what was close to the heart of the Master, then listen to those final words before His departure. All four writers of the Gospels took note, as did Luke in the Acts of the Apostles: Matthew 28:19, 20; Mark 16:15, 16; Luke 26:46, 47; John 20:21; Acts 1:8."

• • •

Gypsy Smith, the famous British evangelist, when asked how he maintained a passion for souls, answered, "Never get over the wonder of it all." Never get over the wonder of Jesus' coming: His birth, life, death, resurrection, ascension and promises. The wonder of His love and the wonder of salvation.

• • •

John Henry Jowett in his book *A Passion for Souls* said, "The Gospel of a broken heart demands the ministry of a bleeding heart."

• • •

"URGENCY:

"If we could sense the heartbeat of God for one moment, it would beat *urgency!*

"If we could read accurately the signs of the times, they would be declaring to us, *urgency!*

"If we could feel the hurts of the people who sit in our pews every Sunday, we would hear the cry of *urgency!*"

• • •

"Every man has a mission, and when we discover what that mission is, we learn that God will endow us for the mission."

• • •

Paul said, "Necessity is laid upon me; yes, woe is me if I do not preach the gospel" (1 Corinthians 9:16).

• • •

Winston Churchill, at the height of the Second World War, challenged his countrymen: "We must do more than our best, we must do what is required."

• • •

E. Stanley Jones, missionary to India for sixty years, gave us words to live by: "Jesus is Lord; Lord of the past, Lord of the present, Lord of the future. Jesus is Lord of everything. Jesus is Lord unqualified. So until the kingdoms of this world become the Kingdom of our Lord and of His Christ, until this Kingdom shall be preached in all the world for a witness, until every last creature has had an option to say what he wants to do about Jesus Christ, let us tell the world that JESUS HAS ALREADY GIVEN US THE VICTORY. Let us go forward in Jesus' Name!"

• • •

Edward Dayton made this statement: "We have no choice but to think of the future, for the future is all that is left of life."

• • •

In Mexico City in 1963, the Commission on World Mission and Evangelism of the World Council of Churches expressed the conviction "that God whose world this is has revealed Himself in Jesus Christ: that all men have a right to know this and those who do know it are committed to making it known."

• • •

The Great Commission is fulfilled! In the schedule of eternity it is already accomplished, the celebration has begun. The question remains: What are we going to do about the Great Commission? Christ's affirmation, mandate, and promise all call for a response. The issues that are addressed do not permit us the luxury of indifference. We must decide.

• • •

David Pawson said, "We try to ignore it, but it won't go away. We attempt to explain it away, but it keeps coming back. Hell is the most offensive and least acceptable of all Christian doctrines. Better to face the truth, even if it hurts."

• • •

Throughout the Bible, when God had a big job to do He often called on a young person.

• • •

William Carey, the father of modern missions, who set sail for India from England in 1793, expressed the conviction:

"When I left England, my hope of India's conversion was very strong, but amongst so many obstacles, it would die, unless upheld by God. Well, I have God, and His word is true. Though the superstitions of the heathen were a thousand times stronger then they are, and the example of the Europeans a thousand times worse; though I were deserted by all and persecuted by all, yet my faith, fixed on the sure word, would rise above all obstructions and overcome every trial. God's cause will triumph."

• • •

"Missions flows from the fullness of God's passion for God and it aims at the participation of the nations in the very passion that He has for Himself. The power of the missionary enterprise is to be caught up into God's fuel and God's goal. And that means being caught up in worship."

• • •

Oswald Chambers said, "The reason some of us are such poor specimens of Christianity is because we have no almighty Christ. We have Christian attributes and experiences, but there is no abandonment to Jesus. Beware of the satisfaction of sinking back and saying 'It can't be done.' You know it can be done if you look to Jesus."

• • •

Peter Beyerhaus said, "We are called and sent to glorify the reign of God and to manifest His saving work before the whole world. Today it is extremely important to emphasize the priority of this doxological aim before all other aims of mission. Our task in mission is to uphold the banner of the risen Lord before the whole world, because it is His own."

• • •

The New Testament makes it clear that God has not left his Great Commission to the uncertainties of the human will. The Lord said from the beginning, "I will build my church." World missions is supremely the work of the risen Lord Jesus.

• • •

Go ye into all the world
Far, far away, in heathen darkness dwelling,
Who, who will go, salvation's story telling
Looking to Jesus, minding not the cost?

• • •

Dr. Paul Bilheimer reminds us that "the fate of the world is in the hands of nameless saints."

• • •

Winkey Pratney said, "Hell sometimes seems to know better than the church the critical nature of the hour."

• • •

Paul Collins declared, "Being in the middle of the road is probably the worst thing you can say about anyone."

• • •

T.E. Lawrence said, "All men dream but not equally. Those who dream by night in the dusty recesses of their minds wake in the day to find that it was vanity. But the dreamers of the day are dangerous men, for they may act their dream with open eyes, to make it possible."

• • •

Dietrich Bonhoeffer: "Our hearts have room for only one all-embracing devotion, and we can cleave to only one Lord."

• • •

Robert Glover: "The missionary enterprise is no human conception or undertaking, no modern scheme or invention, no mere philanthropy even of the finest kind. It did not originate in the brain or heart of any man, not even William Carey, or the apostle Paul. Its source was the heart of God Himself and Jesus Christ, God's great missionary to a lost world—the supreme revelation of His heart and expression of His love. The one great fact in which all true thoughts of God must find their root is the fact of John 3:16, which is the very heart of the Gospel and the central biblical text for missions."

• • •

"The measure of God's love for the world was the value of the gift He gave to save it."

• • •

"If there had been no commission," Professor W.O. Carver said, "or no obedience to its spirit, there would have been no need for the New Testament writings and no occasion for their production. A product of missions, the New Testament can be truly interpreted only in the light of the missionary idea."

• • •

"One of the most important things leadership must accomplish is to give their congregations a genuine vision of the vast scope of need throughout the world."

• • •

"Missionary work is sacrificial, difficult, dangerous and exacting. But we must never allow it to become merely the human activity of the propagation of the 'letter' of the word.

New Testament missionary ministry is to be made 'glorious' and more 'glorious' by the Spirit of glory.

• • •

Missionaries are ordained to preach, trained to teach and to heal, skilled to win savage races for Christ; but every method is to be subordinated to the one great message of the remission of sins through faith in His blood.

• • •

"Obedience to Jesus Christ is essential, but not compulsory; He never insists on being Master."

• • •

Winston Churchill defined a fanatic as "someone who can't change his mind and won't change the subject."

• • •

"God has young people hidden in His quiver who will emerge in the twenty-first century as great international leaders of the body of Christ," declared David Shibley.

• • •

The Amsterdam Declaration: "The records of evangelism from the apostolic age, the state of the world around us today, and the knowledge of Satan's opposition at all times to spread the gospel, combine to assure us that evangelistic outreach in the twenty-first century will be an advance in the midst of opposition.

• • •

The Millennial Manifesto: "We abandon ourselves unreservedly to Him and to His cause. In do so, we know we will risk incurring the wrath of a world that rejects us even as it rejected and crucified Him. Yet His Great Commission is not merely an option to be considered, but a mandate to be obeyed. Therefore, in light of His Second Coming, we covenant together, by God's enabling grace, to strive toward the goal of the whole church taking the whole Gospel to the whole world."

ABOUT THE AUTHOR

Thomas Paino, Jr. is Executive Director of ActioNow, a support team of business people working with Assemblies of God missionaries. He has visited over 60 countries on behalf of missions. A pastor for 50 years, he led his home church in Indianapolis, Indiana, for 38 years, Lakeview Church, which became one of the top three churches in the denomination in missions giving.

Dr. Paino served on the board of the Foreign Missions Department and was a member of the Decade of Harvest committee. He served 15 years on the board of Evangel University, and was chairman of the board of Romania Bible University in Bucharest for 14 years. He is a board member of Evangel Theological Seminary in Kiev, Ukraine. He was President of Indianapolis Teen Challenge for nine years and was Executive Presbyter for the Indiana District of the Assemblies of God.

Thomas Paino and his wife, Lois, of 63 years, have five children, 12 grandchildren and 10 great-grandchildren.